Human Centered Organizational Culture

This book is part of the Human Centered Book Trilogy, the 2021 volumes of the Routledge Human Centered Management HCM Series. HCM books are pioneering transformation from the traditional humans-as-a-resource approach of the industrial past, to the humans at the center management and organizational paradigm of the 21st century. HCM is built on talent and wellbeing of people in the workplace driving work engagement, quality standards, high performance and productivity for long-term organizational sustainability in the global VUCA (volatile, uncertain, complex, ambiguous) environment.

This book was carefully crafted by recognized international human centered scholars from four continents. Although all organizations seek to have an optimal culture, unstoppable disruptions in the VUCA environment easily derail even the best efforts. Conventional assumptions of culture as a unifying organizational force are hardly defendable today. HCM maintains that culture is not only about cohesiveness and consensus but effective management of conflict and disagreements continuously testing the capacity of people to work together. This book is about organizational transformation positioning people at the center. Complementary chapters integrate as antidotes to overcome disruptions in the VUCA environment and the effects of the COVID-19 pandemic affecting people and organizations worldwide.

This and its two complementary titles *Soft Skills for Human Centered Management and Global Sustainability* and *Sensible Leadership: Human Centered, Insightful and Prudent* are timely readings for leaders, managers, researchers, academics, practitioners, students and the general public responsible for organizations across industries and sectors worldwide pursuing quality standards and organizational transformation to attain sustainability.

Maria-Teresa Lepeley is President and CEO of the Global Institute for Quality Education, USA.

Oswaldo Morales is Associate Professor of Administration in the ESAN Graduate School of Business at ESAN University, Peru.

Peter Essens is Director of the Center of Expertise in the Department of Human Resource Management and Organizational Behavior at the University of Groningen, The Netherlands.

Nicholas J. Beutell is Professor of Management in the LaPenta School of Business at Iona College, USA.

Nicolas Majluf is Emeritus Professor in the School of Engineering at Pontificia Universidad Católica de Chile.

Human Centered Management Book Series

The purpose of the book series is to re-position people to be at the center of organizations, the economy and society. Using management as the common denominator, the ultimate goal is to perform a paradigm shift from the entrenched approaches of the industrial past to a human-centered methodology which is convergent with the needs of people and organizations in the constantly changing interconnected world that frames the new Knowledge Society.

The challenges that management is facing when dealing with human development, active participation, responsible leadership, financial accountability, and social responsibility issues can only be understood and solved through the cross-fertilization of ideas from different disciplines. Better integration between management, psychology, neuroscience, economics, education, business, and others, needs to happen to accrue the benefits. The reason is simple. Global conditions create increasingly complex problems that can be highly disruptive. Solutions require approaches that build resilience through embedding multidisciplinary models that are effective in building productive organizations, transparent markets, sustainable economies and inclusive societies.

Maria-Teresa Lepeley, Peter Essens, Nicholas J. Beutell, Book Series Editors

Other Books in the Series

Human Centered Management
5 Pillars of Organizational Quality and Global Sustainability
Maria-Teresa Lepeley

Rethinking Leadership
A Human Centered Approach to Management Ethics
Roland Bardy

Wellbeing for Sustainability in the Global Workplace
Edited by Paola Ochoa, Maria-Teresa Lepeley, Peter Essens

The Wellbeing of Women in Entrepreneurship
A Global Perspective
Edited by Maria-Teresa Lepeley, Katherina Kuschel, Nicholas J. Beutell, Nicky R.M. Pouw and Emiel L. Eijdenberg

For more information about this series, please visit:
www.routledge.com/Human-Centered-Management/book-series/HUMCM

Human Centered Organizational Culture

Global Dimensions

Edited by
Maria-Teresa Lepeley,
Oswaldo Morales,
Peter Essens,
Nicholas J. Beutell,
Nicolas Majluf

Routledge
Taylor & Francis Group
NEW YORK AND LONDON

First published 2021
by Routledge
605 Third Avenue, New York, NY 10158

and by Routledge
2 Park Square, Milton Park, Abingdon, Oxon, OX14 4RN

Routledge is an imprint of the Taylor & Francis Group, an informa business

Library of Congress Cataloging-in-Publication Data
Names: Lepeley, Maria Teresa, editor.
Title: Human centered organizational culture : global dimensions / edited by Maria-Teresa Lepeley, Oswaldo Morales, Peter Essens, Nicholas J. Beutell and Nicolas Majluf.
Description: New York, NY : Routledge, 2021. | Series: Human centered management | Includes bibliographical references and index.
Identifiers: LCCN 2020046637 (print) | LCCN 2020046638 (ebook) | ISBN 9780367551117 (hbk) | ISBN 9781003092025 (ebk) Subjects: LCSH: Corporate culture. | Organization. | Human capital.
Classification: LCC HD58.7 .H844 2021 (print) | LCC HD58.7 (ebook) | DDC 658.3/12--dc23
LC record available at https://lccn.loc.gov/2020046637
LC ebook record available at https://lccn.loc.gov/2020046638

ISBN: 978-0-367-55111-7 (hbk)
ISBN: 978-0-367-55112-4 (pbk)

Typeset in Sabon
by MPS Limited, Dehradun

Contents

Foreword by the Editors of the Human Centered Management Book Series

The book *Human Centered Management: 5 Pillars of Organizational Quality and Global Sustainability* (Lepeley, 2017) that launched Routledge's HCM Book Series in 2017 is a compendium of decades of experience validating conditions that determine the long-term sustainability of organizations in all industries and sectors present in the global VUCA (volatile, uncertain, complex, ambiguous) environment. Worldwide organizations that achieve standards of quality and excellence and become most competitive in terms of high performance, productivity and economic success, achieve these standards with systemic and systematic improvement, only possible because the people who work in and for these organizations demonstrate high levels of work engagement on a daily basis invariably driven by these organizations' efforts to secure the wellbeing of their people in the workplace.

Maria-Teresa Lepeley, a quality management researcher and practitioner, has had the unique opportunity to observe these results first-hand as an examiner of the Baldrige National Quality Award of the United States, and adviser to NQAs Programs in Chile, Brazil, Peru, Colombia and Ecuador, and related NQAs Programs in Europe. Lepeley's background in economics, management, education and entrepreneurship endorses the value of multidisciplinary approaches to find organizational solutions in complex environments in the 21st century. Her studies align with those of Human Centered Management scholars and authors of 15 of the 25 most influential management books of the 20th century recorded by the Academy of Management (Bedeian and Wren, 2001). Among them, Edwards Deming, Douglas McGregor, Abraham Maslow, Chris Argyris and Elton Mayo.

Lepeley's development of her Human Centered Management model consolidated when early in the 2010s she addressed the subject with Peter Essens. With a PhD in social sciences with extensive research on how people work, organize and collaborate to solve complex problems in organizations in diverse industries and sectors, including the military, Essens led key investigations in effectiveness within and between teams and organizations. Coming from different academic and international backgrounds, Lepeley and Essens found a strong common ground that high-performing organizations in the global VUCA environment always position humans at the center: people are the engine.

Lepeley founded the Human Centered Management Book Series supported by the enthusiasm that a visionary Routledge editor, Rebecca Marsh, had on this emerging management field. In 2018, the Series added the book *Rethinking Leadership: A Human Centered Approach to Management Ethics*, by Roland Bardy. In 2019, *Wellbeing for Sustainability in the Global Workplace* was edited by Paola Ochoa, Maria-Teresa Lepeley and Peter Essens. In 2020, *The Wellbeing of Women in Entrepreneurship: A Global Perspective* was edited by Maria-Teresa Lepeley, Katherina Kuschel, Nicholas J. Beutell, Nicky Pouw and Emiel Eijdenberg.

As Book Series editor Nicholas J. Beutell has made a major contribution to position the wellbeing of working people at the apex of Human Centered Management. A professor of management, business administration and healthcare management, former Dean of the Hagan/LaPenta School of Business at Iona College, Nicholas also has a background in quality management, and he developed the quality teams at Iona College leading to the AACSB accreditation. His areas of research include work–family issues affecting small business and entrepreneurship, entrepreneurial intentions and wellbeing with an extensive record of national and international publications.

Under the human centered editorial guidance of Maria-Teresa Lepeley, Peter Essens and Nicholas J. Beutell, the Routledge *Human Centered Management* Book Series has experienced substantial growth, which in a short period of time exceeds a hundred contributors, steering attention to human centered scholars around the world.

In this instance, the *Human Centered Trilogy* of books is enriching the Series with simultaneous publication of three complementary management subjects in leadership, organizational culture and Soft Skills. The books are titled *Sensible Leadership: Human Centered, Insightful and Prudent,* authored by Nicolas Majluf and Nureya Abarca; *Human Centered Organizational Culture: Global Dimensions,* edited by Maria-Teresa Lepeley, Oswaldo Morales, Peter Essens, Nicholas J. Beutell and Nicolas Majluf; and *Soft Skills for Human Centered Management and Global Sustainability,* edited by Maria-Teresa Lepeley, Nicholas J. Beutell and Nureya Abarca.

In this Trilogy, the talent and experiences of Majluf, Abarca and Morales add significant value to advance the HCM Book Series aimed to continuously enrich the wellbeing of Human Centered Management followers and readers worldwide.

MTL PE NJB

Preface by the Book Editors

Since the publication of *Human Centered Management: 5 Pillars of Organizational Quality and Global Sustainability* in 2017, the inaugural book in the Routledge Human Centered Management Series, the number of volumes has grown exponentially, propelled by the interest and contributions of over one hundred scholars from around the world.

This *Human Centered Organizational Culture: Global Dimensions* book is part of a Trilogy of Human Centered Management books. This innovative Trilogy was coordinated to address the mounting and unavoidable challenges confronting organizations in the global volatile, uncertain, complex, ambiguous (VUCA) environment from a comprehensive variety of angles. This book is complementary with other two volumes entitled *The Human Centered Leader: Sensible, Insightful and Prudent* and *Soft Skills for Human Centered Management and Global Sustainability*. The three books are published simultaneously to bridge persistent gaps in traditional resource-focused management formulas that are no longer effective to solve complex problems requiring human centered solutions in management and organizations.

Human Centered Management (HCM) is embedded in the wellbeing of people as a precondition for consolidating human centered culture in the workplace. Clarifying that wellbeing is a personal characteristic affected by the satisfaction of human needs and work in an environment that fosters collective wellbeing leading to increasing organizational performance and productivity. Wellbeing does not exist in a vacuum. It emerges from human centered leadership and organizational cultural models that value wellbeing as a condition for organizational thriving.

The scholars contributing chapters in this book are highly aware of the pressing need for cultural transformation in organizations. To advance this transformation, HCM acknowledges the challenges leaders and organizations face. HCM realizes that no culture can please everyone or that every person can fully identify with the organization's culture.

Although most organizations work to attain an optimal culture that unifies the beliefs and behaviors of its members, all confront unstoppable disruptions and unprecedented diversity that hallmark 21st-century organizations with high potential to obstruct the best efforts. Therefore, the conventional idea of culture as a unifying force that brings people together to work productively toward the attainment of organizational goals can be misleading in the VUCA environment. Organizational culture is no longer about cohesiveness and unity but also about disagreement, discrepancy and disparities. Culture is continually testing people's capacity to work together using their emotional intelligence to optimize benefits by undertaking efforts to reach shared and ethical organizational goals, despite individual differences.

Consequently, agile organizations are promoting cultures of experimentation. Numerous chapters in this book support experimentation. These models provide alternatives for culture transformation with higher potential to optimize wellbeing. Such workplaces focus on human capital, the talent of people, stimulating curiosity, using sensible and prudent leadership, promoting autonomy, experimentation and valuing work engagement and encouraging active participation in innovations at all levels of the organization.

Human Centered Management aims to move organizational cultures forward and advancing a better future recognizing the importance of investing in effective training for employees' development. In times of high uncertainty, it is challenging to formulate organizational strategies that are absent of risks. Under these conditions, leaders need to support co-workers to take educated risks to succeed, dissuading risk aversion that obstructs change and perpetuates the status quo, eliciting dynamic connections between future prospects and present actions to help people and the organization.

Moreover, the post-coronavirus (COVID-19) pandemic environment has exposed human beings worldwide to extraordinarily challenging and unprecedented circumstances in 2020. Human centered leaders and managers need to recognize that people may be experiencing different kinds of grief and anxieties to deal with surmounting disruptions and maintain focus on the continuous assessment and improvement necessary to consolidate the Human Centered Organizational Culture in times of peril. This book offers a diversity of human centered approaches to deal with the need for experimentation and continuous improvement of organizational culture. The cases are empowered by the experiences of 28 scholars from 5 continents gathering an outstanding multi-dimensional international mosaic that covers a broad spectrum of themes. Their contributions range from practical models aimed at enhancing people's wellbeing and stimulating work engagement leading to high productivity to conclude with a theoretical review of the evolution of organizational culture in the last seven decades and the pending missing human centered focus. The variety of Human Centered Organizational Culture solutions presented in the book includes sustainable quality management, a life–work continuum, a social complexity model, a culture model framed for knowledge-intensive organizations, a virtuous-culture supporting people with disabilities, challenging cultures in business organizations, assessment of cultural inter-organizational collaboration and effects of disruptions in cultures in healthcare organizations confronting COVID-19 pandemic.

The editors commend the efforts and innovation of chapter authors whose pioneering work is elucidating Human Centered Management and Human Centered Organizational Culture. All recognize that the need for transformation is long overdue, and all these chapters offer valid and stimulating options for change.

We value the interest and growing demand of a global audience seeking solutions for fostering cultural change contingent on people's wellbeing, which kindled the idea of producing this book.

We thank the support of our families, colleagues and friends around the world that inspired and challenged us to undertake the great work that has implied the production of this book. We firmly believe that our Trilogy will add significant value to the Routledge Human Centered Management Book Series.

We hope that you, our readers, enjoy and benefit from this new human centered journey fostering continuous improvement of organizational culture as much as we have enjoyed and benefited from this unique global and collegial, collaborative experience.

MTL OM PE NJB NM

About the Book Editors

Maria-Teresa Lepeley President and founder of the *Global Institute for Quality Education*, a research think tank focused on quality-based solutions for human centered organizations integrating education excellence with high-performance workplaces in the Knowledge Economy. She is an economist, educator and entrepreneur. Quality Management specialist author, trainer, speaker and examiner of the US Baldrige National Quality Award and adviser to NQAs Programs in five countries in Latin America. She holds M.S. in Economics (economic development) and M.A. in Education (Higher Education Management and Leadership) from the University of Miami, US, B.S. in Education and English from the University of Santiago, Chile. She was Director and Professor of Executive Management Programs at the University of Connecticut, US and at the Department of Economics, School of Business and Economics, University of Chile, and President of Entrepreneurial College in Santiago, Chile. She is a Founder and Principal Editor of Routledge's *Human Centered Management* Book Series and Information Age Publishing Book Series Innovation in *Human Centered Sustainability*. Authored books: *Human Centered Management: 5 Pillars of Organizational Quality and Global Sustainability; EDUCONOMY. Unleashing Wellbeing and Human Centered Sustainability; EDUQUALITY. Human Centered Quality Management in Education. A Model for Deployment, Assessment and Sustainability, and Management and Quality in Education. A Model for Assessment.* She is co-editor of the *HCM Routledge Series books Wellbeing for Sustainability in the Workplace. A Global View and The Wellbeing of Women in Entrepreneurship* and Palgrave Macmillan book *Human Centered Management in Executive Education.* She is author and coauthor of numerous journal articles in quality management, economic development and entrepreneurship. She is an examiner of US

Baldrige National Quality Award, an adviser to National Quality Award Programs in five Latin American countries.

Oswaldo Morales Associate Professor in Management at the ESAN Graduate School of Business, ESAN University, Lima, Peru. He holds PhD in International Studies from the Graduate School of Asia Pacific Studies, University of Waseda, Japan and an MBA from ESAN, Peru. He has a Master's degree in Economics and Public Service Regulation from the University of Barcelona, Spain, a Master in Business Law from the University of Lima and Law Degree from the University of Lima, Peru. His areas of interests include administration and organization, intercultural management, strategic analysis, competence development and entrepreneurship. His multidisciplinary experience allows him to approach human capital development from a creative perspective, focusing on generating value.

Peter Essens Director of the Center of Expertise of HRM and Organizational Behavior at the Faculty of Economics and Business, University of Groningen, The Netherlands. He received his PhD from the Radboud University of Nijmegen, The Netherlands. His research focus is on how people work, organize and collaborate to master complex problems in settings with multiple actors. He has over 25 years of experience in the functioning of people and organizations in diverse domains, including the military. Peter has been leading key investigations in effectiveness within and between teams, and organizations, interaction processes. His recent work has been published in leading journals including the *Journal of Occupational and Organizational Psychology*, *Journal of Management Studies*, *Journal of Organizational Behavior* and the *Academy of Management Journal*. He is an editor of the Routledge Human Centered Management Book Series and co-editor of the book *Wellbeing for Sustainability in the Global Workplace*.

Nicholas J. Beutell Professor of Management, Business Administration and Healthcare Management at Iona College, New Rochelle, NY, US. For a decade, he was Dean of the Hagan/LaPenta School of Business at Iona. He served as acting dean at Stillman School of Business, Seton Hall University. He developed a quality management team at Iona leading to the AACSB accreditation. He has been a consultant for Equitable Life Assurance Society, Public Service Electric and Gas and AT&T. He developed and ran a successful internet business for 17 years. His main areas of research include work–family issues affecting small business and entrepreneurship, entrepreneurial intentions and wellbeing. He is an active member of a research group on work–life issues among entrepreneurs. He is co-editor of a special issue on work–family issues in South Asia for the *South Asia Journal of Business Studies*. He is author of the book is *Evaluating Scholarship and Research Impact* (Emerald) and co-editor of *The Wellbeing of Women in Entrepreneurship* (Routledge). He is a widely cited author; his publications have appeared in the *Academy of Management Review*, *Journal of Vocational Behavior*, *Journal of Small Business and Entrepreneurship* and the *Journal of Managerial Psychology*, among many others. He is a member of the Academy of Management, Eastern Academy of Management and Work Family Researchers Network.

Nicolas Majluf Emeritus Professor of Engineering Management at the Catholic University in Chile (PUC). He holds an Engineering degree from the Catholic University of Chile PUC, an MSc in Operations Research from Stanford University and a PhD in Management at MIT Sloan. He was the Deputy Dean of the School of Engineering and Academic Director at PUC. He is currently the Academic Director of online management courses *Clase Ejecutiva* in Chile. His academic career moved from Strategy and Finance to Organizational Behavior. He is author of four books and many papers on strategy with MIT Professor Arnoldo Hax, and co-author of a widely cited article on finance with MIT Professor Stewart Myers with over 25,000 citations in Google Scholar. He has written books on Human Centered Management and Business Ethics. He has been a visiting professor at MIT Sloan, the Anderson School of Management at UCLA and IESE in Barcelona. He has ample professional experience as a consultant and as board member in foundations and many large Chilean public corporations. He has received numerous awards and academic recognition for excellence in teaching and research.

List of Contributors

Armand Bam directs Social Impact at the University of Stellenbosch Business School and is Senior Lecturer in Business in Society on the MBA program. He holds a PhD in Business Administration from the University of Cape Town with his thesis titled *Embodying virtue in employment: Exploring the employment experiences of people with disabilities*. In 2019, he was the lead author of the paper titled *Transformative learning through social engagement: Reflections on responsible leadership development in management education* that received the Best Paper Award at the International Business Conference 2019. He has over two decades of experience in the non-profit sector developing his practical experience on people-centered management.

Paul Barach, MD, MPH, Wayne State University School of Medicine, Detroit; Jefferson College of Population Health, Philadelphia, USA; Sigmund Freud University, Vienna, Austria. MD, MPH, (Maj (ret.). He is a double boarded anesthesiologist and critical care physician-scientist. He has been Chief Medical Officer and Associate Dean of leading academic medical centers and startup companies. His areas of expertise include patient safety, strategy, clinical model development and redesign, physician leadership and engagement, performance and quality improvement. He is a Clinical Professor at Wayne State University School of Medicine, Lecturer and senior advisor to Dean, Jefferson College of Population Health. He trained at the Massachusetts General Hospital. He holds adjunct academic professorial appointments in Universities in Europe, Africa and Australia. His work has led to over $14,000,000 in competitive grant funding and he has published more than 300 scientific papers and 5 books.

Lorenzo Cobianchi is an Associate Professor in General Surgery at the Department of Clinical-Surgical, Diagnostic and Pediatric Sciences, University of Pavia, Italy. He graduated *magna cum laude* from the University of Pavia where he also obtained the Specialty in General Surgery with honors, and the PhD in Microsurgery and Experimental

Surgery. He was a Postdoctoral Fellow of the Miller School of Medicine, University of Miami, where he received the *Award of Excellence for Outstanding Fellowship*. Besides his clinical research topics about mini-invasive surgery, oncology, new integrated approaches for the treatment of pancreatic cancer and regenerative medicine, he is interested in the impact of new technologies on surgery and healthcare, knowledge translation and co-production in medicine and surgery.

Francesca Dal Mas is a Lecturer in Strategy and Enterprise at the Lincoln International Business School University of Lincoln, Lincoln, UK and Honorary Research Fellow at the Sapienza University of Rome in the Dipartimento di Diritto ed Economia delle Attività Produttive. She has a Bachelor's and a Master's degree in Business Administration from the University of Udine, Italy, a Law degree from the University of Bologna, Italy, and a PhD in Managerial and Actuarial Sciences from the Universities of Udine and Trieste, Italy. She is an international assessor for the MIKE – Most Innovative Knowledge Enterprise Award for Italy and Iran. She was a visiting fellow and a guest lecturer at several universities in Japan, Russia, Italy, Australia, Hong Kong and Iran. She has authored several papers in the field of strategy, intangibles and sustainability.

Maria Ferrara is a Post-Doctoral Associate at the Department of Psychiatry, Yale University, School of Medicine, New Haven, CT, US; Program for Specialized Treatment Early in Psychosis (STEP), Connecticut Mental Health Center, New Haven, CT, US. She graduated *magna cum laude* from the University of Modena and Reggio Emilia (Italy) where she also completed her residency in Psychiatry. She led the development of an assertive outreach based coordinated service for first-episode psychosis in the Province of Modena. Since 2017, Dr. Ferrara has been the research coordinator for the implementation and analysis of the NIH-funded STEP-ED project that includes a campaign to reduce the duration of untreated psychosis. Dr. Ferrara authored several scientific papers and book chapters regarding population health-based efforts for psychopharmacology, first-episode psychosis, interventions for women´ mental and physical health, psychopharmacology and HIV Psychiatry.

Ignacio Ferrero is Dean of the School of Economics and Business and Professor of Business Ethics at the University of Navarra. He holds B.S. degree in Philosophy and Economics and PhD degree in Economics from the University of Navarra. He has published several books on Business Ethics and articles in academic journals. He is working on virtue ethics and the common good in finance, and motivations at the workplace.

Neena Gopalan is an Associate Professor at the School of Business, University of Redlands, California, US. She teaches in MBA and MS in Organizational Leadership programs. She is Associate Director of the Banta Center for Ethical and Purposeful Leadership at the School of Business. Her research interests include leadership, work–family interface topics related to understudied segments of population, including immigration/immigrants. She is keen on collaboration on these topics and is currently involved in multiple related projects.

Vishal Gupta is Associate Professor in Organizational Behavior at the Indian Institute of Management, Ahmedabad, India. He teaches and conducts research in leadership development, emotions, emotional intelligence and mindfulness. He serves as the President of the Indian Academy of Management, affiliate of the US Academy of Management. His research has been published in journals including *Academy of Management Journal*, *Human Resource Management*, *International Journal of Human Resource Management* and *Personnel Review*, and it has been covered by Indian national dailies including the *Times of India*, *Economic Times*, *Business Line*, *Ahmedabad Mirror*, *Mint* and *DNA*. He serves as independent Director on the Board of Gujarat Gas Limited, India's largest City Gas Distribution Company.

Katherina Kuschel is an Associate Researcher studying and teaching innovation and entrepreneurship at CENTRUM Graduate Business School and Pontificia Universidad Católica, Peru. She holds PhD in Social Psychology from Universitat Autònoma, Barcelona, Spain. She was Assistant Professor of Management at the School of Economics and Business, Universidad del Desarrollo, Chile. She has conducted extensive research on women in entrepreneurship as Research Associate at Universidad Tecnológica Metropolitana, Chile, Lazaridis School of Business and Economics, Laurier, Canada and University of Siegen, Germany. Her research focus in entrepreneurship includes women founders of technology ventures, motivations on business startups in STEM, role of women in ecosystems, teams and identity building as women founders, and securing capital for startups. She is the leader of the research group on work–life issues among entrepreneurs. Guest editor at the *International Entrepreneurship and Management Journal* on Women Entrepreneurship in STEM. She is chapter author and co-editor of Routledge book entitled *The Wellbeing of Women in Entrepreneurship: A Global Perspective* (2019/20) which is part of the Human Centered Management Book Series led by María Teresa Lepeley.

Rossella Lucà is a full-time Scientific Researcher at the Institute of Biochemistry and Cell Biology at the National Research Council (CNR), Rome, Italy. She graduated *magna cum laude* from the University of Rome Tor Vergata as Molecular Biologist, and obtained her Ph.D. in Biomedical Science – Mechanisms for human disease – at the Catholic University of Leuven, Belgium. Her research focuses on studying the mechanisms of cancer progression to translate it in the development of preclinical models for high throughput and tailored anti-cancer drugs therapy. Her scientific work is published in several high-quality scientific journals and is part of it is a registered patent. Dr. Lucà is also a project manager and scientific writer for Horizon 2020-SME instruments and reviewer of several peer-review journals.

Maria Francesca Manca is a public health specialist currently working at the Regional Health Agency of the French Overseas Department of Mayotte. She graduated *magna cum laude* from the University of Milan. She later moved to France in order to specialize in public health at the University of Bourgogne in Dijon, France, where she obtained her Specialty with honors. She has a Master degree in public health from the University of Lorraine, France and a Master degree in international relations from the University of Lyon, France. She works as a public health practitioner on epidemics prevention and management. Besides infectious diseases, she is interested in health promotion and community health.

Mirko Modenese is working at Humco s.r.l. – A.I. Cognitive integrator & Data Analysis, Venice, Italy. He has 20 years of experience in the use of self-learning algorithms of computational statistics (ML/NN) in different fields: medicine, genetic epidemiology (degenerative neurological diseases), statistical quality control in production (six sigma approach). Graduated in computer science and statistics, he specializes with a Ph.D. in biostatistics/genetic epidemiology as a researcher at the European Academy of Research of Bolzano, Institute of Biomedicine. Today, he maintains an interest in health and business research by implementing and adapting identified machine learning algorithms for the optimization of the production processes of goods and services.

Sergio Morales is a Research Assistant in ESAN University. He is Bachelor of Anthropology from the Major National University of San Marcos, Lima, Peru and Master student in Epistemology at the Major National University of San Marcos, Lima, Peru. He has published scientific papers in journals in Peru, Argentina, Spain, Colombia and UK. His areas of specialization include topics such as methodology and epistemology of anthropology, cognitive anthropology, evolutionary theory and organizational theory.

Jan Willem (J.W.A.) Nuis is a Senior Lecturer in Strategic Human Resource Management at CHE University of Applied Sciences in Ede, The Netherlands and Ph.D. candidate at Nyenrode Business Universiteit. His main area of expertise lies in the field of people management, social complexity and dialogic HR. He lectures in strategic and sustainable HRM and change management in several bachelor and management courses. He is a member of the CHE UAS research group researching innovative ways of organizing meaningful relationships between organizations and individuals, including employment relationships. He is Chair of the Curriculum Committee overseeing both content and structure of people management courses. Besides his academic position, he is also a self-employed consultant, trainer and coach in people and change management.

Pascale Peters, PhD, is a Full Professor at the Center of Strategy, Organization and Leadership of Nyenrode Business Universiteit, the Netherlands. Her main area of expertise lies in sustainable people management, flexible working and flexible work arrangements, home-based teleworking and New Ways of Working, work–life balance, boundary management, gender, time use, empowerment and leadership. She has published on these themes in edited books, book chapters and articles in among other journals in *Human Relations, Work, Employment and Society, Human Resource Management, Equality, Diversity and Inclusion, International Journal of HRM, Community, Work and Family* and *Small Business Economics*. She is also involved in peer reviewing and acts as expert, consultant, researcher and subcontractor in national and EU-wide projects.

Daniele Piccolo, BAEng, MD, Neuroscience Department, University of Padova, Padua, Italy. He has degrees in Engineering and Medicine from the University of Udine, Italy. He is the founder and Chief Executive Officer of Nucleode Srl, an innovative start-up company in the field of technology and healthcare based in Gorizia, Italy. He was research fellow at Northwestern University in Chicago and University of Pittsburg, USA. In addition to being an entrepreneur Daniele is a Neurosurgery Resident at the University of Padua, Italy and author of publications linking medicine, technology, and management.

Javier Pinto is an Assistant Professor of Business Ethics and HR Management at Universidad de los Andes, Chile. He holds Ph.D. in Philosophy from University of Navarra, Spain. He has published several articles on theory of work, business ethics and human resource management. He is currently working on virtue ethics and the common good theory of the firm related to employment and managers' fiduciary responsibilities.

Gareth Rees is Professor at ESAN University teaching undergraduate and postgraduate courses. He holds Ph.D., MBA and Mcom degrees from the University of Otago, New Zealand. He has publications on Peruvian entrepreneurship, culture and organizational performance and Lean Thinking in healthcare.

Gabriele Romani Direzione Medica Presidio Ospedaliero, Public Health, Azienda AUSL, Modena, Italy. He graduated in Medicine and Surgery at the University of Modena and Reggio Emilia; he later obtained the

Specialization in Hygiene and Preventive Medicine from the University of Milan. He is qualified for the functions of the chief in Occupational Medicine. He is the Head of the Medical Management of the Pavullo Hospital within the Modena Health Agency, Italy.

Linda Ronnie is an Associate Professor of Organisational Behavior and People Management at the University of Cape Town's School of Management Studies, South Africa. She holds Ph.D. in Education (UCT), MEd (Sheffield) and MSc (Applied Psychology). Her research interests include the attraction, retention and motivation of talented, capable employees in diverse contexts and the role of psychological contract shaping individuals' working lives. Prior to her academic career, she worked in the manufacturing sector where she gained extensive management experience. A committed and enthusiastic management educator for 20 years, she was presented with the prestigious UCT Distinguished Teacher's Award in 2014.

Germán Scalzo is Professor of Business Ethics at Universidad Panamericana, Mexico. He holds Ph.D. in Government and Organizational Culture from University of Navarra, Spain. He has published numerous articles, chapters and books on the relationship between economics, business and ethics based on anthropological and philosophical dimensions. His current research includes personalist virtue ethics and the logic of gift.

Susanne Täuber is Associate Professor of Organizational Behavior at the University of Groningen, Faculty of Economics and Business, The Netherlands. She received her PhD from the Friedrich-Schiller University in Jena, Germany. Susanne's research examines the role of social identity processes during organizational change, particularly in mergers. She investigates factors that obstruct the translation of policy into actual organizational change in the context of gender quotas and workplace health programs. Susanne's research was funded by a prestigious VENI grant from the Dutch Research Foundation. Her work has been published in leading journals including the Journal of Management Studies, Organizational Behavior and Human Decision Processes, and Nature.

Frederik Wermser is PhD candidate of Organizational Behavior at the University of Groningen, The Netherlands. His research activities focus on social identities, intergroup relations and culture during collaborative organizational change. In his Ph.D. research, Frederik studied soldiers' reactions and longitudinal integration of German and Dutch army units using surveys and interview techniques. Frederik has been invited as guest speaker in leadership seminars and has been a presenter at the Academy of Management Conference.

List of Figures

List of Tables

Part I

Human Centered Models of Organizational Culture

1 The Human Centered Sustainable Quality Culture in Organizations

Maria-Teresa Lepeley

Why Organizations Need a Human Centered Culture and Quality?

In the article *Creating a Culture of Quality,* Srinivasan and Kurey argue that quality has never mattered more than today (2014). Indeed, although quality management (QM) and standards emerged over half a century ago, they were first used in manufacturing as a systematic method to attain continuous improvement to produce products without errors, waste and miscalculations to satisfy the needs of clients and avoid returns. But today quality is the most meaningful advantage organizations pursue across industries, sectors and in countries worldwide. It is for all to see that technology has strengthened organizations but overall has empowered customers to seek information and compare ratings of products and services about quality problems, and unhappy customers use social media extensively to broadcast complaints having a direct impact on organizations' performance, competitiveness and sustainability.

These are some of the visible features of quality-seeking organizations. But quality is a complex construct with roots engrained in a paradigm shift required to ensure the success of the organizational transformation to meet the demands of the Information Age and the Knowledge Economy. In this environment, approaches of the industries that consider human being as just another organizational resource – which are perpetuated in the labels HR, HRM and SHRM – are no longer effective and are harming people in the workplace and obstructing quality attainment. HR is doomed and due for a major overhaul. This chapter discusses causes and effects leading the quality transformation and the consolidating Human Centered Management (HCM) and the Human Centered Organizational Culture (HC OC).

In my book *Human Centered Management. The 5 Pillars of Organizational Quality and Global Sustainability* (Lepeley, 2017), I provide a systemic model to support the organizational transformation from the humans-as-resources approach to the humans-at-the-center paradigm. HCM is built on QM principles anchored in human capital, and the talent of people in the organization deploys resilience and agility (Lepeley, 2021b) to secure wellbeing in the workplace as a precondition to satisfy the demands of customers to optimize benefits and minimize costs of unavoidable disruptions in the global volatile, uncertain, complex and ambiguous (VUCA) environment and attain long-term sustainability. The purpose of this chapter is aligned with the main principle of this book: HC OC bloom when people thrive. This is the main quality principle.

The chapter is divided in 3 parts. The Introduction discusses the causes pressing the organizational culture transformation and the need to advance from the humans-as-resources HR locus of behavior to the humans at the center HC imperative. The second part discusses the importance of people's wellbeing in HC OC and introduces a multidimensional approach integrating the traditional inward-looking approach with the outward vision as condition for quality and sustainability in the VUCA environment. The third part discusses the integration of HCM quality component that is shaping the human centered quality culture in organizations. The chapter closes identifying elements pressing for change and the costs associated with postponing the culture transformation.

What is Organizational Culture?

Organizational culture may be compared to the *personality* of an organization. It represents the tacit foundations encompassing values, ethical principles, assumptions and behaviors, which originally were established by the organization's founders. Organizational culture commonly shows familiar clues followed by the people who work IN and FOR the organization.

A word of advice is to understand an important difference between working IN and FOR an organization. Although IN and FOR are commonly used interchangeably, HCM calls attention to special differences that mark level of commitment and work engagement that drive performance, productivity and, actually, organizational success and long-term organizational sustainability. Stating that people work IN an organization implies they work and receive a salary for the work they deliver, but it does not necessarily mean they work also FOR the organization. In HCM, FOR requires high commitment with job responsibilities and work engagement. Clarifying that work engagement can only be achieved when workers, regardless of their position in the organizational chart or level or responsibility, feel genuinely happy with the job they do on a daily basis and stimulated to put their best efforts to achieve continuous improvement as individuals and as members of the organization.

HCM highlights the importance and implications of work engagement as an essential element of organizational success and sustainability and it is a critical factor pressing for the transformation of organizational culture. HCM is also aware of the challenges organizations face in order to shape a culture that pleases all and where every person feels included and can be identified with the organization. Whereas organizational cultures tend to unify beliefs and behaviors of its members, the unprecedented diversity in organizations of the 21st century hinders achievements.

Among other unprecedented disruptions, increasing life expectancy of people brings together up to five different generations to the workplace. This unparalleled phenomenon generates new challenges for organizations that complicate the search for solutions and expose need to find new formulas.

Traphagan tackles the challenges. In his 2017 HBR article *We're Thinking about Organizational Culture All Wrong*, he posted that the study of organizational culture commonly conveys the idea of culture as a unifying force that brings people together to work productively toward the attainment of organizational goals. The approach implies that organizational culture is understood as a collective project able to create unity and cohesion in some simple steps. But reality presents a quite different picture because today culture is not only about cohesiveness and unity. It is also about disagreement, discrepancy and disparities constantly testing the capacity of people to work together and benefit advancing common and ethical organizational goals in spite of individual differences.

In HCM, the foundations of an effective organizational culture are built on the continuous search and identification of common grounds aligned with the wellbeing of people in work environments that mirror inclusive societies working for the common good. Culture is shaped by behavioral forces that people use to expedite the achievement of goals. The closer these forces align with organizational pursuits, the better it is for the organization and its members.

Scope of the HC OC Transformation Challenge

The global surveyor Gallup, in its 2017 *State of the Global Workplace*, reported gloomy results of work engagement. Approximately 15 percent of employees surveyed worldwide expressed they feel engaged with work, compared with 85 percent not engaged or actively disengaged. It is important to highlight that global surveys have limitation and overlooking some important dimensions of work engagement including cultural differences (Kathirasan, 2015) but can help to understand overall situation. Among them the inferences reported by one of the authors of the study, Jim Harter, Chief Scientist of Workplace Management and Wellbeing at Gallup, concluded that these results show a sign of global mismanagement (2018). This confirms the perception and critical calling for deeper assessment and organizational improvement embedded in quality standards.

Gallup calculated the economic consequences in lost productivity in approximately US$7 trillion, not to mention the huge costs in human disappointment and frustration. In view of this, Harper stated that the majority of the workforce not engaged or disengaged with work are not the worst performers but are workers indifferent to the organization and unwilling to support its mission (2018). Although these people give their time to an organization (in exchange for a salary), they are not stimulated to make their best efforts or share their best ideas to advance the organization. In short, it can be inferred that a significant portion of workers worldwide work IN but not FOR the organization.

As far as the human dimension is concerned, whereas most likely these workers at one point in time were willing to make a difference in the organization, most likely nobody noticed their talents or expressed interest in human capital and relevant talents they could provide to improve the organization and got discouraged and detached.

Concerns are growing about the work engagement issues coming from multiple disciplines. Some experts emphasize that organizations are overlooking essential elements of employee wellbeing (Pfeffer, 2018). Recent studies conducted at Harvard University are examining why employee initiatives fall short of human centered expectations (Harvard Business Review, 2020).

The interest on work engagement research has grown steadily since last decade (Schaufeli & Bakker, 2010, Schaufeli, 2012, Schaufeli, 2018) along with expanding exploding studies on happiness that have grown from organizations to the national level (Lepeley, 2017) and international comparisons (Helliwell et al., 2020). Drastic disruptions in the global VUCA environment in 2020 are igniting rapid need to explore organizational culture transformation and new non-traditional approaches.

Accelerating the Transition to HC OC

In the year 2020, while we are producing this and two other complementary books that will be part of a Human Centered Trilogy, people and organizations worldwide are affected by unprecedented disruptions caused by the COVID-19 pandemic. At the beginning of the year, the coronavirus has exposed the world to high health risks due to the spread of infection changing the life and work routines of people worldwide. People quarantined at home for months and increasing numbers of deaths worldwide are also challenging the survival of organizations and industries forced to closing restrictions. The pandemic effects are leading nations into deep contraction of national economies and deterioration of the social strata across societies.

Although this pandemic may not be inducing a need for organizational culture transformation, it is certainly accelerating concerns for a change. Today, there is widespread awareness of management challenges pressing organizations to switch traditional work standards from office work to distance home-based work for millions of workers. In this precarious volatile global environment, organizational cultures with resource-based rigid structures are exposed to drastic consequences and considerable losses.

An article by Stefan Thomke in the March–April 2020 issue Harvard Business Review is highly consistent with ideas I discuss in this chapter. The title is *Building a Culture of Experimentations. It takes more than good tools. It takes a complete change in attitude* (Thomke, 2020). The lessons conveyed highlights that a culture of experimentation is timely for organizations to prepare for the post-COVID-19 reality. It emphasizes that the main obstacles obstructing change are lodged in the culture, in deep shared behaviors, beliefs and values that shape a culture over time and perpetuate in place without periodic or effectiveness assessment and in spite of obsolescent outcomes. Thomke posts that a successful culture of experimentation is built on 5 critical elements: cultivation of people's curiosity, insisting that data trump educated opinions (avoiding guessing), democratize experimentation across organizational divisions, promoting ethical sensitivity in all functions and embracing a humane and agile leadership model (2020). At this point in time, experimentation aimed to transform organizational culture is no longer an option for organizations seeking sustainability, it is an imperative.

HCM: The Paradigm Shift

Decades of experience in management research, teaching, training and consulting in QM led me to develop the model and write the book *HCM* (Lepeley, 2017). The purpose of HCM is to substitute the humans-as-resources approaches created during the industrial age that are exacerbated by the pandemic and the global VUCA environment.

The urgency to put people at the center of organizations positions HCM as a timely and effective alternative to speed the transformation to solve HRM shortcomings. Ulrich and Dulebohn in their article *Are we there yet? What's next for HR?* (2015) observe that in the last three decades, HR advanced from a low-level administrative and maintenance function to a core business model. But they query if HR has arrived at its final destination, observing that HR is still deeply entangled in the humans-as-resource slant of the past industrial revolution. The intrinsic nature of HR is blocking organizational culture transformation.

Ulrich and Dulebohn point to flaws, obsolescence and conformity obstructing the need for revision and improvement of a model that was useful in the past but is harming organizations today. The inward-looking human-as-resource HR approach was conceived a century ago when the industrial revolution was at full speed and new industries needed workers to advance the production of machines and manufacturing. HRM principles were galvanized in the US by Frederick Taylor's theory of Scientific Management (1911) and in Europe by Max Weber's framework for bureaucratic organizations (1922). Up to date, the hierarchical resource-based principles and bureaucratic practices persist in the Human Resources offices, and its derivative acronyms HR, HRM and SHRM are still used in organizations, academics and business schools worldwide. But today HRM, more than a realistic meaning, exposes comfort with the status quo, risk aversion to innovate and lack of capacity to assess shortcomings.

I do not minimize or dismiss the outstanding contributions of Taylor and Weber to advance management in the 20th century. On the contrary, I recognize that their models were paramount to step up national production from the precarious agricultural prototype to the industrial setting allowing well-structured organizations that accelerated prosperity, economic growth and national development in countries around the world. But it is crucial to point out the differences a century makes. At the beginning of the 20th century, resources were limited and scarce, money and capital were scant and the emerging workforce needed plenty of workers to fill in production lines and organizations, largely in manufacturing. Most importantly, the level of education of the population was low to nil and skilled workers were extremely rare. Today, these characteristics have reversed, but HRM has prevailed in spite of serious shortcomings obstructing the transformation to HCM.

HCM is Not New, But Humans-as-Resources Management is Stubborn and Difficult to Change

Historic records of the American Academy of Management (AoM) include Taylor's 1911 book *Principles of Scientific of Management* and Weber's 1922 book *Theory of Social and Economic Organizations* among the 25 most influential management books of the 20th century (Bedeian & Wren, 2001). Their work was a major accomplishment that expanded the benefits of the industrial revolution to nations worldwide. But the shortcomings of the human-as-resources HR focus surfaced almost a century ago. The first scrutiny evolved from the Hawthorne Studies (1927–1932) conducted at Western Electric Company plant in Chicago, Illinois by Elton Mayo, an Australian psychologist, organizational theorist and professor of Industrial Research at Harvard School of Business Administration. He made important contributions to advance social psychology and business management, and pioneered multidisciplinary strategies to solve increasingly complex human challenges in organizations. Mayo's 1933 book The *Human Problems of the*

Industrial Civilization is also included in the AoM list of most influential books of 20th century. Mayo was among the first theorists showing concern for the wellbeing of human beings in the workplace as a fundamental aspect to increase performance and organizational productivity.

In addition to Mayo's book, the AoM's most influential management books include 15 management books emphasizing the human wellbeing focus (Bedeian & Wren, 2001). Actually, the majority of the most influential management books of the 20th century focused on people and showed concern for wellbeing in the workplace. These management books provided core support and are embedded in theories I developed to build the HCM model.

Given this evidence, it is puzzling to see why it is taking so long for organizations to advance transformation from HRM to HCM as a necessary condition to attain sustainability. The fact is that the human centered approach is not new, but human-as-resource tactics are deeply entrenched and risk-averse managers and organizations fail to focus instead on the wellbeing of people to optimize investments in resources in a sustainable fashion.

Identifying Differences between HRM and HCM and McGregor Theory X and Theory Y

In 1960, Douglas McGregor published one of AoM's masterpieces: *The Human Side of the Enterprise.* Six decades later, his model is as sound as then to illustrate differences between HRM and HCM, so I use it to clarify the most critical aspects involved in the transformation that are also at the core of QM. Table 1.1 contrasts characteristics of the HR model ascribed to Theory X (left) with HCM features associated with Theory Y.

Hierarchy of Power Differences in HR and HC Organizational Culture

Differences between HRM and HCM affect the sources of power that drive organizations and their culture. Whereas the sources of power in HRM are embedded in bosses, ad hoc with hierarchical bureaucratic organizations that enforce strict controls on subordinate workers, in flat structured HCM organizations, human centered leaders work at building trust aiming to foster co-workers autonomy and delegation of personal responsibility in the execution of their tasks as a necessary condition to stimulate creativity and innovation essential to advance in the VUCA environment. Differences between sources of power in HRM and HCM culture and leadership are presented in Tables 1.2 and 1.3.

Table 1.1 Characteristics of HRM Model Ascribed to Theory X and HCM Features Associated with Theory Y

Theory "X" HRM	Theory "Y" HCM
People do not like to work	People like to work when they feel motivated and engaged with work
Most people think work is an inconvenience	People like to assume responsibilities
People only work to earn income to live	People feel proud of their good works
It is necessary to force people to do their jobs	People feel glad to work in a stimulating environment
People avoid responsibilities	People value to be trusted and feel responsible
It is necessary to control people constantly to perform their work	Clear guidelines and freedom incentive people to perform effectively and be engaged with their work
The most effective method to induce people to work is to increase their sense of security and threaten them to lose the job	People are encouraged to advance organizational mission in stimulating workplaces where individual and collective wellbeing of workers, regardless of rank, are the main features linked to values, responsibility, teamwork and easy access to information flow, and when leaders and supervisors offer AFFECTIVE and effective support to expedite continuous improvement leading to quality standards.

Source: Lepeley, 2017, p. 29.

Table 1.2 Sources of Power in HR and HC Organizational Cultures

Sources of Power common in HR	Features
Coercive powerSource: coercion	Command over others controlling information or imposing difficulties
Enticement powerSource: monetary or material compensation	Command over others based on compensation for special favor
Position powerSource: position in organization	Based on responsibility of a position
Expert powerSource: Knowledge, experience.	Granted by personal capacity and knowledge
Sources of Power common in HCM	Features
Genuine powerSource: Emotional Intelligence.Constructive Leadership. Quality culture.	Mentorship, mutual respect built on trust, empathy, understanding and capacity to create synergy with other people

Source: Lepeley, 2001.

Table 1.3 Contrasting Power Structure of HR Bosses and HC Leaders

HRM bosses	HCM leaders
Focus on processes	Focus on people
Use control	Inspire trust
Follow short-term goals	Aim at long-term benefits
Focus on finding problems	Focus on finding solutions
Perpetuate status quo	Incentive innovation
Favor repetitive activities	Promote change for continuous improvement
Follow rules and fair change	Foster autonomy with responsibility for achievement
Intolerant of failure and experimentation	Take failure as steps to improvement
Follow destructive competition[1]	Promote constructive competition[2]
Command actions	Pursue Win–Win negotiation
Emphasis on hard skills	Emphasis on Soft Skills[3]

1 Destructive competition: One winner takes all.
2 Constructive competition: win-win competition.
3 Lepeley, M. T. (2021). Soft Skills for Human Centered Management and Global Sustainability.Source: Lepeley, 2001.

HRM is Controlled by Bosses. HCM is Boosted by Leaders

Differences in sources of power shape different styles to manage people in the organization. Leaders in HCM organizations deploy *genuine sensible power* embedded in emotional intelligence to provide constructive guidance and support the efforts of people in the organizations to systematically achieve continuous improvement and quality standards. Table 1.3 presents contrasting characteristics of bosses as superiors and chiefs' characters in humans-as-resources organizations with leaders who serve as guides and mentors in the human centered culture.

These comparisons clarify differences in sources of power in HRM that tend to overestimate the impact and effects of physical resources at the expense of quality standards and the wellbeing of people in the workplace emphasized in HCM driving high-performance and long-term sustainability in the Knowledge Economy. This contrasting feature exposes causes in losses in productivity leading to mismanagement as highlighted by Harper above affecting work engagement around the world.

Preeminence of Human Wellbeing

In HCM, the wellbeing of people in the workplace is a critical organizational force leading transformation to the human centered culture. The concept of wellbeing needs clarification because it has numerous interpretations that can be misleading.

In HCM, wellbeing is a multidimensional concept and requires understanding of complementary and differences between personal wellbeing and organizational wellbeing.

Wellbeing is commonly used as a synonym for happiness, but this interpretation is inconsistent with HCM. In HCM, personal wellbeing refers to a sustainable state of individual fulfillment resulting from an adequate balance of six interactive life dimensions anchored in satisfaction of human needs that are essential to find the purpose of life. The satisfaction of human needs is aligned with Maslow's theories (1954), but instead of a hierarchy of need, in HCM, human needs are constantly interacting, developing and strengthening each other in purpose of a life purpose. In HCM, personal wellbeing evolves from the Aristotelian eudaimonic principle where a person assumes responsibility for continuous self-improvement as a precondition to be able to help other and contribute to improve society. Based on this principle, quality education becomes a central component of human wellbeing (Lepeley, 2019a, b). HCM wellbeing contrasts with happiness which is understood as a short-term personal feeling of pleasure and avoidance of pain related to Epicurean hedonic arguments.

PERSONAL WELLBEING

In HCM, personal wellbeing is embedded in a balance of 7 life dimension components compiled to find the purpose of life as shown in Figure 1.1. The 7 life dimension components are described below.

Figure 1.1 The 7 Complementary Interactive Life Dimensions.

Life purpose as equivalent to a life compass and a driver to make wellbeing attainable and sustainable
Freedom, autonomy basic human attribute in the pursue of wellbeing
Physical fitness responsibility to secure good health and fitness
Income to secure financial independence to cover life expenses and enjoyment
Love and affection are critical foundations of meaningful relationships, emotional support and empathy.
Contribution to society to secure shared, collective, attainable and sustainable wellbeing in the workplace and inclusive societies.
Intellectual long-life learning sustains brain activity, alertness as source of stimulus throughout life. Spiritual growth prepares for life enjoyment and to face death as a natural stage of life.

WORKPLACE WELLBEING

Wellbeing in the workplace refers to the organization's capacity to reach quality standards and a culture based on trust and ethics where leaders and employees feel satisfied with the work environment and the social relationships. Wellbeing at work is an essential aspect in the HC OC and a central area of concern to achieve quality standards that secure organizational sustainability and business success.

All books in the Routledge Human Centered Management Series are driven by people's wellbeing. I cover the subject in my book *Human Centered Management: The 5 Pillars of Organizational Quality and Global Sustainability (2017).* We added two books addressing wellbeing of working people titled *Wellbeing for Sustainability in the Global Workplace* (Ochoa, Lepeley, & Essens, 2018) and *The Wellbeing of Women in Entrepreneurship* (Lepeley *et al.*, 2020). The HCM books cover a broad spectrum of the disruptions and challenges affecting wellbeing and provide insightful solutions to help people who work IN and FOR organizations as employees and as entrepreneurs, in the case of our book on women entrepreneurs.

Understanding the Dimension of the Wellbeing Challenges in the Global Workplace

To put in perspective the wellbeing challenge for organizations and working people, it helps to have an idea of the magnitude in numbers.

The International Labor Organization (ILO) reports that the global workforce reached 3.3 billion in 2019. Latest report by Wikipedia in 2012 shows that the global workforce was approximately 3 billion workers employed in the businesses and the productive private sectors and about 200 million people were unemployed and actively seeking employment. The 2017 Global Entrepreneur Monitor reported that in the 65 countries surveyed, the number of entrepreneurs working on their own reached 582 million. The number of employees in the public sector is far more difficult to calculate. In fact, ILO reports public employment in percentages of the workforce by country instead of numbers. Across countries, the average percentage of people employed in the public sector is approximately ¼, but there is a wide variance. Cuba, Russia and China have the highest percentage ranking from 70 percent to 50 percent, respectively, in 2013. In the same year, Hong Kong with 8 percent and Japan with 11 percent showed the lowest proportion of people employed in the public/government sector. A rough estimate of 5 billion people worldwide are working (approximate 60 percent of the total world population).[1] The implications for management and organizational culture are staggering.

Addressing Organizational Culture and Wellbeing Challenges

The traditional analysis of employees' wellbeing has been addressed in psychology on issues mainly related to stress, employees' relations, safety and mental health. In the last decade, wellbeing in the workplace is attracting a lot of scholars in organizational culture, management and leadership observing the effects of workloads, leaders and managers' styles, impact of financial dimensions, trust in working relationships, work autonomy and work–life balance, among others. Routledge Human Centered Management Book Series includes two books dedicated to the analysis of wellbeing in the workplace: *Wellbeing for Sustainability in the Global Workplace* (Ochoa, Lepeley, & Essens, 2018) and *The Wellbeing of Women in Entrepreneurship* (Lepeley et al., 2020).

LIFE–WORK CONTINUUM: THE NEW HUMAN CENTER ORGANIZATIONAL CULTURE

HR approaches to organizational culture consistently segment human life in work activities and personal life endeavors, concentrating on life at work and underscoring fundamental aspects of personal wellbeing. Concerned about the effects of pending work–life imbalance, Beutell, Kuschel, and Lepeley (2021) wrote a chapter for this book introducing a theoretical life–work continuum model as an alternative organizational culture. The purpose is to substitute the traditional HR segmenting work–life analysis as opposite dimensions of a person's life for an integrated method to assess wellbeing. We argue that the present work–life formulas need deeper scrutiny to include workers' wellbeing (Beutell et al., 2021).

CONSOLIDATING HCM THROUGH SUSTAINABLE QUALITY STANDARDS

In previous sections, I proposed to advance the human centered paradigm to replace HR management approaches of the industrial age that fail to meet organizational demands today. In this context, I emphasized the importance to deploy management formulas targeting the wellbeing of people as precondition to optimize work engagement, performance and long-term sustainability. A rough estimate of the billions of workers affected showed the dimension of the challenge ahead. I stressed the positive correlation that exists between human wellbeing and sustainable quality standards underlying HCM. In the next section, I examine these links, which, in my view, expose the main differences between HCM and HRM and the need for transformation.

QM is Alignment of the Inward and Outward Dimensions of Organizations

As an economist with a background in education and business management, I had a clear understanding of the *interdependence* between supply and demand, the only law in economic theory. Supply representing people who work in organizations that produce and provide (sell, deliver) products and service to customers. Demand representing customers, clients, users or people with needs and to satisfy them buy products from suppliers/organizations in the productive private sector. But the same principles apply to users who receive services produced and delivered by organizations in the public/government sector (paid indirectly through taxes). From this description, it is clear that organizations (supply) exist only if they have customers, clients, users (the demand) who seek/buy products/services the organization produces. Otherwise, organizations have no reason to exist.

The importance of customers is paramount in economics. But it is also a rational aspect of management. So, when I studied management, I was puzzled to see that traditional management theories were anchored in HRM related exclusively to the supply side of the equation but ignored the critically important demand side. Management was based on an inward-looking vision of organizations (supply) that ignored the critical outward vision (demand) and its effects on sustainability. In the 21st century, technology and the increasing numbers of disruptions affecting organizations in the VUCA environment are pressing organizations to complement inward and outward visions as a necessary condition to attain quality standards.

My concern about the segmented management vision focused on HRM principles increased when I specialized in quality management. My first encounter with QM took place when I was the Director of the Miami Chapter of the National Association of Business Economist where I met fellow economists who worked for the Florida Power and Light Company. This was the first American company that won the Japanese Quality Deming Award[2] in 1987. This was my quality initiation. Since then, I have worked consistently in quality management. I wrote the first QM book applied to education in 2001 published by McGraw-Hill. Quality education and quality principles *applied* to education are critical conditions to facilitate the deployment of quality standards in the workplace. Systematic approaches to quality improvement induced me to write *Human Centered Management: The 5 Pillars of Organizational Quality and Global Sustainability* (2017) to address quality and sustainability challenges in organizations. The following section provides a summary of the quality movement history to explains the central role of quality embedded in the Sustainable Quality Management (SQM) pillar of my HCM model.

DEMING'S TOTAL QUALITY MANAGEMENT (TQM) PROPELLED BY HUMAN WELLBEING

Edwards Deming is recognized as the Father of Quality. His 1982 book *Quality, Productivity and Competitive Position* is included in AoM list of *the* most influential management books of the 20th century. I value Deming's TQM model, his influence in global quality developments has impacted the culture of organizations worldwide for the last three decades. Deming was the main influence in the creation of National Quality Awards (NQA) in nations around the world. Quality and the pursuit of excellence are anchored in people's wellbeing in organizations. I was an examiner of US Baldrige NQA and adviser to NQA programs in Chile, Brazil, Colombia, Peru and Ecuador.

Deming introduced to management the missing outward-looking organizational dimension. The new quality approach turned around the traditional inward-looking vision conventional in HRM. Deming challenges organizations to focus on customers, in the community where customers come from and in society at large. Adding the outward-looking vision, Deming pioneered the concept of organizational and corporate social responsibility.

A WORD ABOUT NQA

Deming's TQM model was used to create NQA programs in countries around the world to increase performance and competitiveness. TQM served as a model to develop the assessment criteria adopted by NQAs after Japan showed outstanding progress in its postwar economy becoming a high productivity nation in less than a decade by deploying quality standards across productive sectors. Japan established the Deming National Award in 1951 sponsored by the Japanese Union of Scientists and Engineers.[3]

US Baldrige NQA Program was established in 1987 to recognize quality accomplishment in manufacturing and business organizations of all sizes that were deploying the quality model and reaching the highest scores certified by trained teams of examiners. In 2001, the Baldrige Award was expanded to recognize organizations in the service sector including education[4] and healthcare.[5] In 2007, Baldrige introduced an award for non-profit and government organizations.[6] I was a member of the Baldrige Board of Examiners between 2002 and 2005 and advocated the creation of the award for non-profit organizations. The Baldrige Awards is administered by the Performance Excellence Program.[7] The European Quality Award was established in 1991, and until today, is sponsored by the European Foundation of Quality Management. Today, more than 80 countries have NQAs to promote high performance, productivity and global competitiveness.

HCM and the Sustainable Quality Pillar

The foundations of the HCM model and its SQM component are summarized in the following arguments. The principles are explicit and shared through the HC OC. HC OC is strengthened with human capital, talent, resilience and agility built in common efforts to attain continuous improvement of organizational performance, productivity and competitiveness driven by constructive and sensible leadership and collaboration practices focused on the wellbeing of people in the workplace. The SQM pillar of HCM fosters an organizational culture encouraging employees' engagement with clarity of individual personal and organizational mission ensuring they work not only IN but FOR the organization. SQM makes the difference between HCM and HRM. In contrast with HRM focused on resources, SQM secures high productivity fortifying first the wellbeing of people. In HC OC, wellbeing is a necessary condition for organization to attain long-term sustainability systematically meeting the needs and expectations of customers and community. The principles in the HC SQM supporting the quality organizational culture are discussed below indicating inward- and outward-looking institutional effects:

- The reason for HC organizations (HCOs) to exist is because there are customers who demand their products and services (outward-looking)
- People who work IN and FOR HCOs feel engaged with work and eager to solve problems with autonomy and supported by leaders who care for the wellbeing of co-workers as necessary condition to attain high performance (inward-looking)
- Constructive sensible leaders in HCOs value and boost human capital and talent to effectively manage resilience (inward-looking) and agility (outward-looking) needed to optimize benefits and minimize costs of disruptions in the VUCA environment (outward-looking)
- Quality teams focused on Talent Management in the selection and development (inward-looking) of personnel in the organization using agility to foster innovation (outward-looking)
- HCM secures integration of the inward–outward dimensions

implementing the SQM Model supporting people and their wellbeing as a condition for sustainability and success.

Srinivasan and Kurey in the article *Creating a Culture of Quality* emphasized how important it is to become competitive today (2014). Quality standards are a significant challenge but meaningful advantages for organizations not only in business but in all sectors. Overall, in government agencies pressed to become more effective and efficient serving the needs of people. And here I need to regress to my experience as an examiner. My proposal to include in the Baldrige NQA Program an Award to distinguish the efforts of non-profit organizations was based on the urgency to include them and integrate the public sector in the national quality initiatives to promote the wellbeing of the population.

Srinivasan and Kurey conducted interviews with leaders of quality teams in 60 multinational corporations and surveyed 850 employees in a wide range of functions and industries at all levels of seniority. They found that traditional resource-based strategies using monetary incentives, training and sharing unprecise and questionable best practices had no effect to reach quality standards. Comparatively, companies deploying human centered and peer-driven approaches showed a stronger quality culture, employees made fewer mistakes and organizations spent significantly less time and money correcting errors. Srinivasan and Kurey define the true culture of quality as an environment where employees not only follow quality guidelines, but consistently recognize the value of teammates working together on actions leading to continuous improvement, hearing others talk about the benefits of quality, and embracing quality as a culture, not as an organization obligation or a hassle.

The 5th HCM Pillar: SQM

In my book *Human Centered Management* (Lepeley 2017), I designed the SQM model based on my experience as an examiner of NQA. I included SQM in HCM to provide a systemic quality assessment methodology accessible to all organizations interested in achieving quality standards, regardless of size, industry, sector or nation, based on the same standards and assessment criteria of excellence promoted by NQAs, which are obtainable only by a small elite of organizations. My intention in SQM is to democratize national quality standards making them available to leaders across HCOs willing to make the efforts necessary to attain world recognized quality standards. I emphasize HCOs because I have not seen any HRM focused organizations attain the aforementioned quality standards.

I simplified SQM application and the evaluation criteria to facilitate access and use of the quality model to people working in organizations of all sizes, including entrepreneurs, to help them reaching out quality standards with significant saving instead of hiring expensive external training and trainers in QM.

SQM is a systemic quality deployment and assessment model. This section identifies the Management Areas (MAs) that impact the culture of HCOs (Lepeley, 2017). To facilitate continuous assessment and improvement, SQM is divided in 7 MAs. Four MAs relate to actions and responsibility of people directly and three MAs assess continuous support to the efforts of people to secure quality standards in the organization (inwards looking) aiming to satisfy customers' needs and expectation and their impact in markets and the community.

Four human MAs

MA1. Focused on the *demand* side of the quality equation: satisfaction of customers' needs and expectations, knowledge of markets.

MA2. Concentration on the *supply* side of the equation: securing high level of work engagement based on employees' wellbeing working IN but also FOR the organization. It identifies merit recognition and continuous training targeting personal growth and talent.

MA3. Human centered leadership supporting the supply dimension. It secures leadership and responsibility for organizational results focused on continuous improvement of people and wellbeing in the workplace as necessary condition to attain quality standards and long-term sustainability that also commits social responsibility with the community.

MA4. Organizational planning: activity coordinating demand (outward looking) and supply (inward looking) components positively effects on the HC OC aligned with systematic quality achievements leading to high performance and long-term sustainability.

Three management quality expeditors

MA5. Use of technology, data collection, synchronized knowledge management and analysis to facilitate evidence-based decisions and efforts to deploy and attain continuous improvement.

MA6. Quality of supporting processes (management of economic, financial and facilities)

MA7. Community integration (vertical and horizontal integration with other organizations, including benchmarking knowledge and activities and environmental care (internal–external).

Each Mas includes five elements of assessment aimed to facilitate data collection, objective measurement and analysis of results, including instruments to assess and to report results and a system to assess progress in performance toward attainment of quality standards.

Prospects and Challenges of the Human Centered Organizational Quality Culture

The shortcomings of HRM are surmounting and the need for transformation to HCM is growing among organizational facing disruptions in the global VUCA environment. There is exponential evidence pressing for change and transformation from HRM to HCM.

The discussion has shown that the need for transformation is high and strong. Yet complacency with the status quo and risk aversion to change and innovate management are strong. Increased awareness of the implications of low work engagement and the costs of mismanagement as the consequences of overlooking the wellbeing of people in the workplace are appalling. A major challenge at hand is the need to create reliable instruments to measure work engagement. This analysis has identified quality key formulas that have a direct impact on organizational cultures to promote people at the center.

I conclude by calling attention to two essential aspects important to strengthen HCOs culture. The first is to recognize and integrate the multidimensional inward-looking scope to conduct an objective analysis of HCOs that impact organizational culture. And the second is to understand that HCM is only possible when efforts are closely aligned with the fundamental principles of QM.

The rough estimates of the number of workers worldwide affected by mismanagement are staggering. This will start motivating more scholars in different fields to join efforts to advance HCM solutions. The diversity of human centered scholars whose chapters are included in this book is a highly encouraging sample of progress in this direction.

I end with a positive note recalling the importance of Thoemke's culture of experimentation and his 5 principles to succeed in cultivating HCM principles: cultivation of people's curiosity, insisting that data trump educated opinions (avoiding guessing), spread experimentation opportunities across organizational divisions, securing ethical sensitivity in all functions and embracing a humane and agile leadership model. Adding that the wellbeing of the people who work IN and FOR the organization is paramount to strengthen the HC OC built on quality standards.

Notes

1 World population estimated is over 7.8 billion in August 2020 https://www.worldometers.info/world-population/
2 Japanese Deming Quality Award https://www.juse.or.jp/deming_en/award/
3 https://www.juse.or.jp/deming_en/award/

4 http://www.nist.gov/baldrige/enter/education.cfm
5 http://www.nist.gov/baldrige/enter/health_care.cfm
6 http://www.nist.gov/baldrige/enter/nonprofit.cfm
7 https://www.nist.gov/baldrige

References

Bedeian, A., & Wren, D. (2001). Most influential management books of the 20th Century, *Organizational Dynamics*, *29*(3), pp. 221–225.

Beutell, N., Kuschel, K., & Lepeley, M. T. (2021). Life-work continuum. The new organizational culture, In M. T. Lepeley, O. Morales, P. Essens, N. Beutell & Majluf N. (Eds.), *Human Centered Organizational Culture: Global Dimensions*. Routledge.

Creech, B. (1994). *The Five Pillars of TQM*. Truman Talley Books/Dutton.

Deming, W. E. (1982). *Quality, Productivity and Competitive Position*. Massachusetts Institute of Technology, Center for Advanced Engineering Study.

Fisher, R., & Ury, W. (1981). *Getting to Yes without Giving In*. Penguin Books.

Gallup. (2017). *State of the Global Workplace*. Gallup Press.

Harvard Business Review (2020). *Why Employees Experience Initiatives Fall Short* Idea Watch. New Research and Emerging Insight. May – August 2020. 15 – 22.

Harter, J. (2018). *Dismal Employee Engagement Is a Sign of Global Mismanagement*. Gallup Organization. https://www.gallup.com/workplace/231668/dismal-employee-engagement-sign-global-mismanagement.aspx.

Helliwell, John F., Layard, Richard, Sachs, Jeffrey & Neve, Jan-Emmanuel De (Eds.). (2020). *World Happiness Report 2020*. New York: Sustainable Development Solutions Network.

Kathirasan, K. (2015). *Employee Wellbeinug in Singapore Workplaces. A New Integrated Approach to Wellbeing Measurements*. UK: Master's Dissertation in Business Administration University of Wolverhapton. https://www.academia.edu/12591422/Employee_Wellbeing_in_Singapore_Workplaces_A_New_Integrated_Approach_to_Wellbeing_Measurements.

Lepeley, M. T., Kuschell, K., Beutell, N., Pouw, N. & Eijdenberg, E. (Eds.). (2020). *The Wellbeing of Women in Entrepreneurship*. UK: Routledge.

Lepeley, M. T. (2021a). Soft Skills for Human Centered Management and Global Sustainability. In M. T. Lepeley, N. Beutell, N. Abarca & N. Majluf (Eds.), *Soft Skills: The Language of Human Centered Management*. US: Routledge.

Lepeley, M. T. (2021b). Master Soft Skills: The Resilience-Agility Umbrella model. In M. T. Lepeley, N. Beutell, N. Abarca, & N. Majluf (Eds.), *Soft Skills for Human Centered Management and Global Sustainability*. US: Routledge.

Lepeley, M. T. (2019a). *EDUCONOMY. Unleashing Wellbeing and Human Centered Sustainable Development*. Information Age Publishing.

Lepeley, M. T. (2019b). *EDUQUALITY. Human Centered Management in Education. A Model for Deployment, Assessment and Sustainability*. Information Age Publishing.

Lepeley, M. T. (2017). *Human Centered Management. The 5 Pillars of Organizational Quality and Global Sustainability*. UK: Routledge.

Lepeley, M. T. (2001). *Management and Quality in Education. A Model for Assessment*. Santiago, Chile: McGraw-Hill Interamerican. (Spanish title: Gestión y Calidad en Educación. Un Modelo de Evaluación).
Maslow, A. (1954). *Motivation and Personality*. Phabhat Books.
Mayo, E. (1933). *The Human Problems of an Industrial Civilization*. New York: Macmillan.
Ochoa, P., Lepeley, M. T., & Essens, P. (Eds.). (2018). *Wellbeing for Sustainability in the Global Workplace*. UK: Routledge.
Pfeffer, J. (2018). *The Overlooked Essentials of Employee Wellbeing*. McKinsey & Company. https://www.mckinsey.com/business-functions/organization/our-insights/the-overlooked-essentials-of-employee-well-being#.
Rath, T., Harter, J. K., & Harter, J. (2010). *Wellbeing. The 5 Essential Elements*. Gallup Press.
Rose, D. (2019). *Why Culture Matters Most?*. Oxford University Press.
Schaufeli, W. B., & Bakker, A. B. (2010). Defining and measuring work engagement: Bringing clarity to the concept, In A. B. Bakker & M. P. Leiter (Eds.), *Work Engagement: A Handbook of Essential Theory and Research* (pp. 10–24). Psychology Press.
Schaufeli, W. (2012). Work engagement. What do we know and where do we go? *Romanian Journal of Psychology*, *14*, 2–10.
Schaufeli, W. (2018). Work engagement in europe: Relations with national economy, governance and culture. *Organizational Dynamics*, *47*, 99–106.
Schein, E. (2004). *Organizational Culture and Leadership*, Third Ed. Jossey-Bass.
Schmidt, E. (2020). In disruptive times, the power comes from people: An interview with Eric Schmidt. *McKinsey Quarterly*. March. https://www.mckinsey.com/business-functions/mckinsey-digital/our-insights/in-disruptive-times-the-power-comes-from-people-an-interview-with-eric-schmidt?cid=other-eml-alt-mcq-mck&hlkid=68c711ff90af444a804b85a40fad6422&hctky=2823006&hdpid=e3a1a525-5484-4aa5-8805-326838e94330
Srinivasan, A., Kurey, B. 2014. Creating a culture of quality. *Harvard Business Review*. https://hbr.org/2014/04/creating-a-culture-of-quality
Traphagan, J. (2017). We're thinking about organizational culture all wrong. *Harvard Business Review*, January.
Taylor, F. (1911). *The Principles of Scientific Management*. Hive Publishing Company.
Thomke, S. (2020). Building a Culture of Experimentation. *Harvard Business Review*. 40–48. March – April.
Ulrich, D., & Dulebohn, J. (2015). *Are we there yet? What's next for HR? Human Resource Management Review*, *25*, 188–204.
Van der Wiele, A., Williams, A. R. T., Dale, B. G., Carter, G., Kolb, F., Luzon, D. M., Schmidt, A., & Wallace, M. (1996). Self-assessment: A study of progress in Europe's leading organizations in quality management practices. *International Journal of Quality & Reliability Management*, *13*(1), 84–104.
Verme, P. (2009). Happiness freedom and control. *Journal of Economic Behavior and Organization*, *71*(2), 146–161.
Weber, M. (1922). *The Theory of Social and Economic Organizations*. Free Press.

2 Life–Work Continuum

The New Organizational Culture

Nicholas Beutell, Katherina Kuschel, Maria-Teresa Lepeley

Introduction to Organizational Culture (OC) in the Workplace

OC is a robust organization dimension that has been extensively researched producing an abundant amount of literature for half a century. Edgar Schein was one of the pioneers focusing on OC (Schein, 1984; Schein, 1990; Schein, 1996; Schein, 2000). In his classic book *Organizational Culture and Leadership* (2017), Schein explains how to transform the abstract concept of culture into a practical tool for accelerating dynamic change, describing what OC is, how it is created, evolves and adapts to contemporary organizational challenges. Tackling the complex question of how to change an existing culture, Schein presents an analytical framework with three OC dimensions: *artifacts and behaviors, espoused values and assumptions.*

All dimensions of OC represent cultural phenomena visible to observers. For instance, the *artifacts* dimension relates to tangible elements of the organization, such as architecture, furniture, dress code, office jokes, all visible elements of a specific OC that can be recognized by insiders, but also by people who are not part of that culture. *Espoused values* refer to organizational values and rules of behavior that are expressed by members that represent the organization to themselves and others. This is often considered as the official philosophies or the public identity statements embedded in the organizational mission and the future vision, the goals that the organization intends to reach. *Shared basic assumptions* are deeply embedded and are considered taken-for-granted behaviors constituting the essence of the OC.

Ehrhart, Schneider, and Macey (2014) have emphasized the need for OC studies by encouraging approaches that integrate external factors influencing OCs with the internal organizational environment. OC research emphasizes that leaders need to effectively manage internal and external elements for OC to drive high performance and improved organizational productivity and long-term sustainability. In contrast with previous OC theories anchored in formal, inflexible structures, the study of OC is accelerating the growth of qualitative analyses emphasizing the human side of organizational life. The rapid growth in demand for effective integration of external pressures and internal organizational responses was precisely what led us to write this chapter. ***Life–Work Continuum: The New Organizational Culture*** proposes to address the shortcomings of Work-Life-Balance (WLB) approaches. The COVID-19 pandemic has affected people and organizations worldwide providing clear evidence that WLB is a cumbersome and unattainable pursuit. New formulas are needed. Thus, the Life-Work Continuum (LWC) proposes the integration of life and work as a holistic continuum aimed at supporting people's wellbeing in the global workplace.

Life-Work Continuum: The New OC

Important changes in societies worldwide have been driving OC transformation. The urgency for change has accelerated as people and organizations are exposed to and suffering from the infectious effects of the COVID-19 pandemic. The OC challenges affecting people and organizations are pending, multidimensional, complex and abundant. To a large extent, the need for change is spurred by organizational environments that facilitate the participation of women in the workforce, help two-career couples manage their lives, support fathers that are assuming increasing amounts of family responsibilities and managing work overload in organizations confronting highly competitive environments. The present conditions are challenging for women and men sharing household and family responsibilities while facing similar career advancement issues and opportunities. Instead of focusing on life and work as separate and mutually exclusive dimensions, the LWC model is a human centered (HC) approach to OC that takes life and work as an integrated whole by connecting human interests, abilities, activities and responsibilities.

Substantial evidence suggests that, to date, few organizations have achieved successful LWC transformation to meet the needs of employees. To a large extent, old OC approaches overlook the complex connectivity of personal life and work life that is only partially recognized or acknowledged in traditional organizations. The entrenched, dichotomous views of the *work–family narrative* (Ely & Padavic, 2020) obstruct the career advancement of women and men by decreasing the wellbeing of working people and lowering work engagement needed for optimal productivity (Lepeley, 2017, Ochoa, Lepeley, & Essens, 2019).

In the case of women, our book, *The Wellbeing of Women in Entrepreneurship* (Lepeley et al., 2020), presents an extensive analysis by global scholars revealing that women entrepreneurs view life–work–family as a continuum, a condition for success and entrepreneurial survival, not as separate dimensions of their wellbeing. Other studies report the similar results (Sehgal, 2020). Most women entrepreneurs perceive their lives in an integrated fashion (Poggesi, Mari, & De Vita, 2017). In short, *life is life*: a holistic, cohesive, *self* image, not a *war of different domains*. Life is a continuous series of events and choices anchored in personal values, beliefs, attitudes and behaviors leading to achievements or failures.

The LWC vision is intended to supplant traditional OCs and academic research approaches where work, family and life are treated as separate and contending "domains" perpetuating the obsolete work–life conflict and balance myths by overlooking growing evidence that a human life is one and needs to be viewed as a seamless, integrated experience for women and for men.

Some issues driving the need to move beyond the traditional WLB approach and recognize the new LWC model for fostering an HC OC in the global workplace include:

- persistent shortcomings in the work–family, work–life dichotomies
- findings supporting synergies between work and family (Beutell & Gopalan, 2019)
- WLB obsolescence perceived by men and women in younger generations (Gen X, Millennials and Gen Z) who do not view life as discrete roles
- evidence that the personal dimension WLB constraints work–life harmony, but it also interferes with productivity and long-term organizational sustainability
- women entrepreneurs, a fast-growing group in the global workforce, are pioneering the need for change.

The chapter addresses these challenges anchored in fundamental Human Centered Management (HCM) principles of human wellbeing aligned with an OC leading to high-performance standards to deal with disruptions in the global VUCA environment.

Evolution of the *Work–Life* Concept

The present limitations of the segmented life–work analytical framework can be traced to the hierarchical resource-centered organizational structure of the first Industrial Revolution (IR). The IR models were designed to meet the demands for labor in industrial societies when workers toiled for long days and received low wages; although conditions have changed, OC schemes have been perpetuated. Change is manifested in new technology and instantaneous communications offering new possibilities for people and organizations worldwide. Yet the legacy of the resource-based OCs, bureaucratic and hierarchical structures with fixed and strict standards continue to drive the separation of work and life (Barnett, 1998).

Paradoxically, in previous agrarian societies, personal life, work and family responsibilities were complementary parts of a life continuum.

But today those factors conflict with forces driving contemporary OCs aligned with the HCM paradigm. Decoupling life into separate spheres in increasingly challenging today. The idea of life segmentation is a myth (Kanter, 2006). Nonetheless, efforts to solve this duality are scarce and overdue yet progress is taking longer than anticipated.

Studies are using different approaches to address the impact of the *work-family narrative*, including a common challenge when women opt to accommodate their work schedules to meet life and family demands instead of striving for top-level organizational positions (Ely & Padavic, 2020). This is happening while men are assuming increasing responsibilities for children, home, caretaking and nurturing, but where their activities are still overridden by career aspirations. This quandary is solvable. Organizations addressing the *life* perspective are using the LWC, focusing on continuous improvement of the wellbeing of people as a necessary condition to stimulate workers' engagement leading to high performance that is essential for long-term sustainability (Lepeley, 2017).

It is important to mention that, although an increasing number of organizations are offering programs on work–life, work–family and flexible work arrangements intended to support workers, many of these programs offered by organizations that purport to address *work–life balance* (WLB) issues, but, in fact, the organization signals family-friendly policies to recruit and retain workers. Employees using such programs may suffer career consequences for actually using these programs. New hires who believe in the value of *work to live*, rather than *live to work*, will soon spot the trick behind an empty signal. Using gimmicks invariably results in negative consequences for organizations.

On the positive side of a negative event, the 2020 COVID-19 pandemic is compelling increasing numbers of organizations to advance LWC as the new OC. Nevertheless, one of the main challenges LCW scholars face is the need to integrate demands at the organizational level with the needs of employees. For organizations, *work equals life* shows little consideration for fulfilling the *life* component of the wellbeing equation. Certain industries and sectors show evidence of a backlash against organizational programs supporting employees with family responsibilities (Perrigino, Dunford, & Wilson, 2018), whether flexible work arrangements or taking of leaves creates conflict among employees, thereby stigmatizing the use of these programs.

COVID-19 is revealing a fresh look at the routines of life. Suddenly, all work in organizations, except for essential services, are mandated to cease, boosting the role of the *life* component as never before in recent human history. Life, work and schooling have been suddenly relocated to home for large segments of society in nations around the world. Beyond the health implications of the pandemic, the economic implications post-COVID-19 are launching an exponential number of uncertainties as the crisis unfolds. One of the most imminent outcomes of the present phenomenon is that life aspect of the work–life formula is becoming transformed with few expectations of that overshadow pre-COVID-19 environment. The multidimensional disruptions caused by COVID-19 are forcing people and organizations alike to recalibrate live expectations, rethink organizational structures and space needs and craft new strategies for the future. And solutions will not come from traditional resource-based approaches of the industrial past but rather from HC organizational strategies that will shape future OCs.

The Emerging *Life–Work Continuum* Culture

OC is the focus of this book. In this context, the LWC OC refers to the shared principles, values, ethics, beliefs, tacit assumptions, behaviors and social interactions that bind organizations to accomplish its mission and vision (Cummings & Worley, 2005; Smircich, 1983). The effects of OC on life–work interactions has been extensively analyzed (e.g., Bailyn, 1993; Lewis, 2001), but not from the HCM perspective addressed in this chapter amid the pandemic environment.

Thompson's work on the impact of OC on work–life interaction (Andreassi & Thompson, 2008; Thompson, Beauvais, & Lynnes, 1999) offers initial guidelines that converge with the HCM model and the Book Series. Thompson and colleagues defined work–life culture as *the shared assumptions, beliefs, and values regarding the extent of organizational support offered to facilitate integration of employees´ work and family lives* (Thompson, Beauvais, & Lynnes, 1999, p. 394).

Three elements were identified in the Thompson studies:

a. Organizational demands for long work hours mean less time for activities and expectations beyond work. Demands for long hours have been increasing including dealing with demanding managers via email, phone, Zoom or other virtual means. In fact, technology is *blurring of the line between work and life which follows the law of diminishing returns. The value derived from the always-on employee can be undermined by such negative factors as increased cognitive load and diminished employee performance and well-being* (Joyce et al., 2018).
b. Some negative consequences associated with use of life–work benefits are analyzed in recent study by Ely and Padavic (2020). This refers to participation in life–work programs that might signal that the employee is wavering on their work/career commitment possibly resulting in negative career consequences. Flexible work arrangements and virtual communications cannot replace the perceived need for face time at the office.
c. Supervisor/managerial recognition of and support for LWC culture. Such managers are in a position to offer life–work support in spite of

specific programs offered by the organization in response to the employee's particular life situation.

One of the reasons organizational life–work programs are not used by employees is because they do not meet LWC needs but follow obsolete traditions of OC. Caproni (1997) argues that work–life initiatives (particularly WLB), and the discourse around them, are manifestations of the logic and language of bureaucratic organizational models that unwittingly reinforce the very models that life–work programs are trying to solve. The antidote to the status quo is *life–work* organization culture based on HCM that recognizes the whole person: that people are adults who want to contribute, engage and grow, who enjoy learning, want autonomy and freedom, make contributions beyond their job descriptions, have lives where work is but one aspect and who reciprocate with the trust and respect extended to them by the organization. Thus, the LWC, placing the wellbeing of employees at the center by fostering engagement and personal growth leading to continuous performance improvement becomes an essential HC culture for organizations to attain sustainability in the VUCA environment.

Generational Expectations and the Life-Work Continuum

For the first time in human history, people from five generations are collaborating in the workplace. To a large extent, the preferences of generational cohorts drive trends in LWC. Currently, Millennials are the largest employee group in the US workforce. Millennials along with Gen Z are visibly pushing OCs increasing the leverage of the LWC more than Baby Boomers did. Younger generations in the labor force value more organizational flexibility that helps them advance their goals, where life interests matter most, and work is but a dimension of their life space.

Millennials show preferences for more work autonomy, fewer job restrictions, recognition, increased focus on performance standards and agile organizations that match their needs that help them to find meaning in their lives. Having a life, rather than climbing a corporate ladder and accumulating assets, is central to the life space of this group. Millennials grew up in the *always on* world so managing life is more seamless for them. The LWC is well-suited to the single largest generation in the US economy.

Zappos Culture: An Example of LWC

Zappos, an Amazon.com company, promotes to have a culture highly appealing to Millennials, and the company has positioned its culture as the corporate centerpiece. Tony Hsieh, its CEO, learned about the critical importance of OC from a previous company he owned where culture turned toxic. He feared going to work each day and the damage was beyond repair. He vowed to avoid making the same mistakes when he created Zappos. In Zappos, he made culture the central focus of organizational mission. Each year, Zappos compiles a culture book showing how OC is enhancing employees' wellbeing and includes opinions of workers about their experience with Zappos's culture. The following quote from Zappos' CEO Tony Hsieh that converges with the HCM approach promoted in this chapter:

> There's a lot of talk about work life separation or balance, Zappos believes in work life integration. *It's just life.* And we consider the ideal when an employee can be the same person at home as in the office. And when people feel comfortable being themselves so creativity can flow and flourish.

Zappos provides employees full-time life coaching to support them in achieving personal and professional goals. Zappos organization is driven by the values embedded in its culture that include: Deliver WOW*!* (impress or excite someone greatly) through service; embrace and drive change; create fun and use imagination, be and act adventurous, creative, open-minded; pursue growth in learning; build open and honest relationships with colleagues using effective communications; build positive work teams and develop family spirit; promote efficiency doing more with less; be passionate and determined and be humble. These values are actionable and unique to the Zappos culture used to hire and, if necessary, fire employees. Zappos reports that the values that underline this OC support employees to be personal and increase performance to satisfy the needs of customers who buy their products and value Zappos service. This is the quote Zappos uses relating to the LWC: *it's just life.*

COVID-19 Pandemic and OC

Deep disruptions caused by the global COVID-19 pandemic are imposing major transformations in human lives and organizations that will have lasting effects in economies and societies. The changing environment has allowed innovative minds to create new concepts for describing dimensions of the current global VUCA environment. One of these concepts is the *low touch economy.*[1] The *low-touch economy* analyzes the effects of the pandemic integrating disruptions of human lives aligned with emerging social and organizational habits. Like never before, the low-touch economy is showing unequivocal clues that confirm the LWC model advanced in this chapter. The low-touch economy concept was developed to describe the new and forthcoming organizational, social and economic scenarios created by social distancing imposed during the COVID-19 pandemic. Going forward, people will have to pay critical attention to changes in personal health habits, restrictive traveling, connecting remotely using virtual and teleworking modes, limited social gatherings and dealing with organizational transformation and decentralization caused by the new social norms for avoiding further COVID-19 infection.

Evidence indicates that organizational and economic solutions will come from HCM approaches able to tackle the LWC instead of deepening the existing segmentation. HC leadership will be a critical component for successful transition to the *new normal.* Furthermore, effective combinations of resilience and agility will be Soft Skills in high demand in HC organizations, among managers and workers seeking to successfully transcend the post-COVID-19 disruptions, by safely navigating the emergent, global VUCA environment (Lepeley, 2021).

Inspiration for the LWC

Our research and studies in human development support assumptions that the LWC will become a stronger *organizational imperative* as consequence of the stay-at-home restrictions during the COVID-19 pandemic. New conditions will press need for transformation of organizations across industries, sectors and nations to conduct a systematic assessment of OC. Organizations failing to recognize that, for most people, work is a part of life rather than as a separate or primary component, will face mounting challenges because this obsolete approach no longer meets the life needs of workers. Moreover, the assumption that working more hours results in immediate increases in performance and productivity is illusory. Long hours and work-overload thwart essentials of wellbeing causing negative effects on physical and mental health, life purpose, family and social life and interference with leisure time increasingly important for unleashing creativity and allowing time for recovery from work. Successful transformation of OC needs to ensure departure from vestiges of the industrial past to guarantee the secure implementation of HCM principles and practices that unequivocally place people at the center of OC (Lepeley, 2017).

Inward-looking OCs endorsing segmentation between life at work and a parallel life outside the workplace will confront increasing challenges in finding talent. Cultural alignment for a unified *life* is essential. To structure the proposed LWC, a vision that strengthens organizational values modeled by HC leaders fosters the engagement of all members of the organization in the collective project. In the HC organization, contrasting with hierarchical and pyramidal structures, leaders are responsible for OC transformation that engages all members of the organization. Majluf and Abarca (2021) in their HCM book, *Sensible Leadership: Human Centered, Insightful, and Prudent*, which is part of this Trilogy, explain that HC leaders foster seamless integration of work life with personal life, emphasizing that segmentation is harmful and affects both work and personal lives. One of the essential characteristics of HC leaders is demonstrating that their lives are consistent with the LWC serving as effective examples of a corporate culture built on an appealing collective mission, vision and values that employees can feel proud to emulate, empowering their decisions and making choices that meet both personal and organizational goals.

Leadership initiatives in HCM project across the organization with continuous assessment of employees' needs and wellbeing, level of engagement and participation as a necessary condition for attaining quality standards aligned with individual merit, as well as personal and collective recognition for special efforts. In the future, needs assessment of people who work for organizations will be embedded in the culture. This includes heightened awareness of generational expectations, from the needs of Baby Boomers (the cohort hardest hit by the coronavirus (COVID-19) pandemic, who are still participating in the labor force, and seeking strategies to optimize synchronization with the needs and demands of coworkers) to Gen X, Millennials and Gen Z). Considering that Millennials and Gen Z comprise nearly half of the world's population, embracing the LWC will be a necessity for OCs.

Looking to a Better Future

We close this chapter by forecasting that the disruptions caused by the COVID-19 pandemic will affect organizations and people so deeply and profoundly that the new normal will be radically different. In the VUCA environment, long-term organizational sustainability, and in reality, survival, will depend on resilience and agility of people and organizations in successfully meeting the needs of a shaken labor force rebounding from this major crisis. In this new environment, it will be impossible to ignore the LWC imperatives addressed in this chapter. Acknowledging the LWC as a necessary improvement in OC for managing omnipresent disruptions in life is essential. Yet, we remain confident that human resilience and agility will create a better future, indeed, better lives. Embracing the LWC will support organizations by enhancing the wellbeing of people in the global workplace required for meeting the complex challenges of the 21st century.

Note

1 Low-Touch Economy. Board of Innovation. https://www.boardofinnovation.com/blog/what-is-the-low-touch-economy/

References

Andreassi, J. K., & Thompson, C. A. (2008). Work-family culture: Current research and future directions. In K. Korabik, D. S. Lero, & D. L. Whitehead

(Eds.). *Handbook of Work-Family Integration: Research, Theory, and Best Practices*. New York, NY: Elsevier.

Bailyn, L. (1993). *Breaking the Mold: Women, Men, and Time in the New Corporate World*. New York: Free Press.

Barnett, R. C. (1998). Toward a review and reconceptualization of the work/family literature. *Genetic, Social, and General Psychology Monographs*, *124*(2), 125–182.

Beutell, N. J., & Gopalan, N. (2019). *Pathways to work-family synergy: resources, affect and wellbeing. Journal of Family Studies*, 1–17. https://www.tandfonline .com/doi/full/10.1080/13229400.2019.1656664.

Caproni, P. J. (1997). Work/Life Balance: You can't get there from here. *The Journal of Applied Behavioral Science*, *33*(1), 46–56. 10.1177/0021886397331003.

Cummings, T. G., & Worley, C. G. (2005). *Organization Development and Change*. Mason, Ohio: South-Western Thomson.

Ehrhart, M., Schneider, B., & Macey, W. (2014). *Organizational Climate and Culture*. New York, NY: Routledge.

Ely, R. J., & Padavic, I. (2020). What's really holding women back? *Harvard Business Review*, *98*(2), 58–67.

Gallup. (2016). *How millennials want to work and live*. Washington, DC. Retrieved from: https://www.gallup.com/workplace/238073/millennials-work-live.aspx.

Joyce, C., Guszcza, J., Fisher, J., & Hogan, S. (2018). Positive technology. *Deloitte Insights*, (April 16). Retrieved from https://www2.deloitte.com/us/en/insights/focus/behavioral-economics/negative-impact-technology-business.html.

Kanter, R. M. (2006). Beyond the myth of separate worlds. In M. Pitt-Catsouphes, E. E. Kossek, & S. Sweet (Eds.), *The Work and Family Handbook*. Mahwah, NJ: Lawrence Erlbaum Associates.

Lepeley, M. T. (2017). *Human Centered Management. The 5 Pillars of Organizational Quality and Global Sustainability*. Human Centered Management Book Series. UK: Routledge.

Lepeley, M.-T., Kuschel, K., Beutell, N. J., Pouw, N., & Eijdenberg, E. L. (2020). *The Wellbeing of Women in Entrepreneurship: A Global Perspective*. Human Centered Management Book Series. London and New York: Routledge.

Lepeley, M. T. (2021). Soft Skills: The lingua franca of Human Centered Management. In M. T. Lepeley, N. Beutell, N. Abarca, P. Essens, & N. Majluf (Eds.), *Soft Skills in Human Centered Management. Global Dimensions*. Human Centered Management Book Series. UK: Routledge.

Lewis, S. (2001). Restructuring workplace cultures: The ultimate work-family challenge? *Women in Management Review*, *16*(1), 21–29. 10.1108/09649420110380256.

Majluf, N., & Abarca, N. (2021). *Sensible Leadership Human Centered, Insightful and Prudent*. US: Routledge.

Ochoa, P., Lepeley, M. T., & Essens, P. (2019). *Wellbeing for Sustainability in the Global Workplace*. Human Centered Management Book Series. UK: Routledge.

Perrigino, M. B., Dunford, B. B., & Wilson, K. S. (2018). Work–family backlash: The "Dark Side" of Work–Life Balance (WLB) policies. *Academy of Management Annals*, *12*(2), 600–630. 10.5465/annals.2016.0077.

Poggesi, S., Mari, M., & De Vita, L. (2017). Women entrepreneurs and work-family conflict: an analysis of the antecedents. *International Entrepreneurship and Management Journal*. doi:10.1007/s11365-017-0484-1.

Schein, E. (1984). Coming to a new awareness of organizational culture. *Sloan Management Review*, *25*(2), 3–16.

Schein, E. (1990). Organizational culture. *American Psychologist*, *45*(2), 109–119.

Schein, E. (1996). Culture: The missing concept in organization studies. *Administrative Science Quarterly*, *41*(2), 229–240.

Schein, E. (2000). Sense and nonsense about culture and climate. In N. Ashkanasy, C. Wilderon, & M. Peterson (Eds.), *Handbook of Organizational Culture & Climate* (pp. xxiii–xxx). Thousand Oaks, CA: Sage.

Schein, E. (2017). *Organizational Culture and Leadership* (5th ed.). Hoboken, NJ, USA: Wiley.

Sehgal, A. (2020). *Work-family interface among women entrepreneurs: Evidence from India. South Asian Journal of Business Studies*, *9*(3), 411–428. https://doi.org/10.1108/SAJBS-11-2019-0213.

Smircich, L. (1983). Concepts of culture and organizational analysis. *Administrative Science Quarterly*, *28*(3), 339–358.

Thompson, C. A., Beauvais, L., & Lynnes, K. S. (1999). When work and family benefits are not enough: The influence of work-family culture on benefit utilization, organizational attachment, and work-family conflict. *Journal of Vocational Behavior*, *54*, 392–415.

Van der Heijden, B., De Vos, A., Akkermans, J., Spurk, D., Semeijn, J., Van der Velde, M., et al. (2020). Sustainable careers across the lifespan: Moving the field forward. *Journal of Vocational Behavior*, *117*, https://doi.org/10.1016/j.jvb.2019.103344a; https://www.sciencedirect.com/science/article/abs/pii/S0001879118300769?via%3Dihub.

3 Cultural Interoperability in Interorganizational Collaborations

Peter Essens, Frederik Wermser, Susanne Täuber

Introduction

What happens when organizations join in a collaboration and form a new collective partnership or alliance? Collaboration is a powerful means for organizations to increase their impact and ensure continued existence. It allows the pursuit of objectives that could not be achieved independently, thereby creating new opportunities. Collaboration typically alters group boundaries and hence affects organizational cultures and identities.

Culture and identity are closely related. Culture refers to shared beliefs, values and collective attitudes of people working together. Culture is communicated through the use of artifacts, such as shared stories, rules, routines, policies and symbols, that guide behaviors of members of a team, organization or nation (Schein, 2009). Multiple cultures may co-exist representing all these different levels and may merge as a complex amalgamation of elements.

Identity refers to a unique set of features of a collective shared by members that distinguishes a collective from others. The stronger individuals relate to the culture of the collective, the stronger the members of the collective define themselves in terms of membership in a particular collective such as an organization (Mael & Ashforth, 1995; Schrodt, 2002).

Because identities and cultures in the workplace form an essential part of people's self-concept, changes due to collaborations can be challenging.

What are the critical conditions for effective collaboration and how can the changes best be managed and prepared for? Advice to prepare and execute collaboration is abundant, with checklists of various lengths. However, these often focus on formal and legal aspects and processes, such as conflict management procedures, and less often on the human and in particular culture-related aspects of collaboration. In this chapter, we provide a framework to assess how cultural differences impact interorganizational collaboration, and how to manage and benefit from such differences based on systematic feedback from participants in the collaboration.

Collaboration and Interacting Organizational Cultures

Collaboration is popular, with new ideas and objectives providing extra energy. However, the complexity of collaboration is often underestimated and therefore failure looms large. Especially due to cultural differences that are typically neglected in the preparation and execution of strategic collaboration with potential to create obstacles building effective cooperation. In other words, Peter Drucker, one of the most influential thinkers on management said Culture *eats strategy for breakfast.*

Effective collaboration rests on the ability and motivation of people of different groups, organizations or nations to work together. People need to bridge differences in thinking and doing, which includes the alignment of often implicit rules and work routines of different organizational cultures which we define as *cultural interoperability* (Wermser, Essens, & Täuber, 2019). It seems logical that people are at the center of collaboration. However, in the preparation and realization of the collaboration, this perspective is often forgotten.

The insights on collaboration and multiple cultures in international contexts outlined in this chapter are based on an extensive number of observations and interactions with military cultures, collaboration, teamwork and civil-military interaction in international contexts (Essens, Vogelaar, Tanercan, & Winslow 2003; De Vries, Walter, Van der Vegt, & Essens, 2014; Essens & Bekkers, 2014; Essens & Thönissen, 2015; Essens & De Vries, 2016; Essens, Thompson, Karrasch, & Jermalavičius, 2016).

The framework and illustrations are based on a study of a strategic collaboration involving Dutch and German military cultures (Wermser et al., 2019; Wermser, Täuber, Essens, & Molleman, 2016; Wermser, Täuber, Essens, & Molleman, 2020). Military organizations are at the forefront of international collaboration of public organizations and have proven to be an invaluable source of inspiration for private organizations (e.g., Kellogg Insight, 2019).

The Distinct Features of Collaborations

Before presenting the critical conditions needed to make collaborations successful, below we differentiate collaborations from other forms of working together. Collaboration is a process where autonomous parties enter into coordinated action to achieve a common goal using an agreed set of shared rules, norms and structures (Wood & Gray, 1991). These new rules, norms and structures form the basis for a collaboration specific culture. In the first place, effective collaboration requires the development of an intentional, strategic and long-term relationship, involving the exchange of information and the sharing of resources, competencies and capabilities. This process creates interdependence between the parties that realize the intended outcomes of the collaboration. Whether the intended outcomes of a collaboration are achieved depends on responsibility fulfillment, accuracy, precision and timeliness of the actions of the partners involved and on the development of a shared culture. Thus, in contrast to coordination and cooperation, collaboration is marked by the closeness and intensity of the relationship (Gulati, Wohlgezogen, & Zhelyazkov, 2012).

Collaborative engagements can vary greatly in size composition, duration, interrelatedness and legal status (see, e.g., Turiera & Cros, 2013). In this chapter, we discuss collaborative engagements as coalitions, alliances and partnerships – conditions of close collaboration with intensive interaction, but where the partners remain legally independent. Managing a collaboration is further different from project management. Unlike projects, collaborations have multiple lines of authority with direct or indirect influence of the sourcing organizations; moreover, collaboration cannot be *ordered*, and people-oriented techniques are needed to motivate participants.

In collaborative engagements, participants bring their cultures stemming from diverse backgrounds, such as groups, organizations and nations, into the collaboration process. This diversity requires special conditions for harmonizing differences to build a collaborative culture. The process of change and learning to work in and with different cultures is critical for success. Careful management where participants provide deliberate feedback on the development of the collaborations is essential for effectively developing the collaboration and achieving cultural interoperability.

Despite collaborators' best intentions, collaboration is a complex and dynamic process with failure rates ranging between 30 percent and 70 percent (Das & Teng, 2000; Kale & Singh, 2009; Thanos & Papadakis, 2012; Park & Ungson, 2001). Sources of failure have been extensively discussed in scientific and popular literature and here are some of them:

- lack of a well-developed or well-communicated shared vision
- lack of clear objectives
- gaps in top management commitment
- an intensive top-down approach
- low engagement of people
- insufficient investment of time and money
- poor governance
- lack of trust
- conflicts of interest
- cultural incompatibility among partners.

Critical Conditions for Effective Collaboration

To resolve the above sources of failure, abundant practical advice has been developed (e.g., Hughes & Weiss, 2007; OECD, 2006), often with a focus on operational formalities. Indeed, formalization of the collaboration with governance agreements and protocols provides structure to collaboration processes which facilitates preventing and solving conflicts. Supporting organizational and technical conditions need to be in place, but culture-related aspects of collaboration, such as motivation, identification, trust and cultural fit, are critical for continued and effective collaboration (Sarkar, Echambadi, Cavusgil, & Aulakh, 2001), yet are often overlooked. People can make collaboration work with a human centered approach (Lepeley, 2017; Ochoa, Lepeley, & Essens, 2019), which is essential for building and maintaining effective interaction required to overcome barriers that emerge in the process of collaboration. The ability to bridge differences is a requisite for exploring and exploiting collaboration opportunities. Bridging differences is essential for creating an organizational culture that places humans at the center of the collaboration process.

Collaborative arrangements are dynamic. Enacting operational processes facilitate emergence of new directions that diverge from the original plan with potential to generate tension between the parties involved. An open orientation to identify and accept cultural differences as new developments and opportunities is a critical component of effective collaboration. Continuous communications and feedback from participants in the collaboration contributes to develop the collective orientation.

Three dimensions of effective collaboration have been identified: partner complementarity, partner commitment and partner compatibility (Sarkar et al., 2001; Mitsuhashi & Greve, 2009; Dhurkari & Nandakumar, 2015). Below, we introduce and use these dimensions as a framework to create an assessment instrument to collect information on critical conditions of cultural interoperability by asking targeted feedback from participants in the collective.

Partner Complementarity

Complementarity relates to a strategic perspective aimed at integrating diverse qualities of the partners, including skills, knowledge, resources, capacities and values. Diversity allows for broadening of the scope of operations, fostering creative synergies and developing new capacities leading to novel and innovative approaches. Complementarity is strengthened with clear and congruent high-level intentions and goals reflecting the combined value of these qualities and the value of the collaboration.

Complementarity is an important criterion for identifying and evaluating the benefits and opportunities of a collaboration. Before initiating a collaboration, assessment of complementarity allows to see whether the collaboration is worth pursuing and prevents ungrounded expectations. In an ongoing collaboration, complementarity questions may assess if the collaboration provides sufficient value addition to balance investment in efforts, time and money.

A strategic review of an ongoing collaboration may lead to the idea that complementarity is not necessarily a stable property of the partnership. Partners may develop and learn from each other, become more similar or develop new ideas and new visions. Moreover, external demands can change and influence the conditions or processes of the collaboration. Such changes may need to update the shared strategic perspective or even the roles partners have in the collaboration (Ring & Van de Ven, 1994).

Partner Compatibility

Compatibility refers to the level of fit between the partners' cultures, operational structures and work routines. Day-to-day practices and routines may be easier to adjust and are less obstructive. Experience tells, however, that simple routines may emerge as surprises for the partners involved. For example, in an operational, civil–military collaboration, the military and the civil parties used significantly different decision-making processes (in military jargon *battle rhythm*) – the military worked in a highly structured manner following routines compared to the smaller civil side, who worked more adaptive to the situation. In such collaboration efforts, finding the optimal alignment is a challenge.

Cultural differences between partners increase the level of uncertainty but may also be perceived as the added value of the collaboration (Meirovich, 2010). Cultural distance, the extent to which different cultures are similar or different, is generally assumed to affect the potential for collaboration (Meirovich, 2010). In the example stated earlier, the military disciplined structure, albeit foreign to the civil partners, helped them to sharpen their routines to the benefit of the collective (Essens & Thönissen, 2015). Thus, whereas routines were different, they were similar enough that it was relatively easy to be aligned in the collaboration.

In the processes of working with multiple cultures, four possible patterns of cultural interaction are identified: *domination, conflict, separation* and *blending* (Schein, 2009).

Domination is a condition where one culture is leading and imposing work structures and procedures in the collaboration. This is often the case when one participant group or sourcing organization is substantially larger or more powerful than the other in the collaboration. Such imbalance may lead to conflict if not recognized and compensated for with equal or at least proportional representation and voice in management.

Maintaining the cultures separately seems logical when the parties remain autonomous, like in the partnerships and alliances discussed here, and rotation of representatives is expected. Still, in order to enable effective collaboration and manage interdependence, agreed set of rules, procedures and shared artifacts are needed.

Creating a collective culture related to the intention of the collaboration leads to some level of blending or integration of cultures. Whereas complete blending of cultures, thereby creating a new culture, may be relevant for new entities, such as a merger, in collaborations where the participants remain representing their sourcing organization may lead to loyalty conflict. It is more likely that separation and blending operate at the same time depending on the need for the collaboration to succeed. In the example mentioned before, the civil and military parties insisted on remaining separate cultures in the collaboration and to be recognized as such. Yet, in order to effectively influence each other thinking and decision-making to address the operational complexity, which is the intent of the collaboration, they needed to develop new, integrated decision-making routines as a *comprehensive approach* (Essens et al., 2016).

Partner Commitment

Commitment is associated with longer term intentions as requisites of time and effort and collaboration-specific resources, such as direct communication lines between sourcing organizations, sharing information, developing and maintaining collaboration. Moreover, commitment is associated with softer aspects such as attention and efforts to resolve obstacles and frictions and celebration of successes, as expressions of commitment. Partners need to demonstrate a balanced sense and perception of each other's commitment, supported by matching actions and recurring communications targeted at advancing collaboration.

While commitments may be assessed and confirmed in agreements and actions, there is always uncertainty about future behavior of the partners. There is a risk that partners deviate from promised or expected behaviors. Accepting the potential risks associated with lack of partner commitment and effectively handling relational uncertainty requires trust between the partners.

Leadership of the partners, representing multiple cultures and identities, has an important role in demonstrating commitment in many ways, such as creating an environment where differences of opinion can be voiced, working to develop a common culture of collaboration, eliciting and combining perspectives of the partners, providing direction in solutions to issues and building trust in the collaboration (Weiss, Anderson, & Lasker, 2002). In multilayered collaborations, the risk of mismatch of commitment at different levels is real and leadership at all levels have to be aligned and active in their role of building and maintaining the collaboration.

Trust is defined as the *willingness to be vulnerable to actions of another party based on expectations that the other party will perform a particular action important to the trustor, regardless of the ability to monitor or control that other party* (Mayer, Davis, & Schoorman, 1995, p. 712).

Trust is initially based on expressed intentions including first impressions, concrete partner behaviors and actions providing the basis for confirmation of expectations. Trust requires sensitivity about what each partner expects, actually perceives and receives. Lack of sensitivity to differences and mistrust commonly result in obstructions, misperceptions and less effective collaboration (Prasanna & Haavisto, 2018). Thus, trust is one of the main factors ensuring continued commitment to collaboration.

The three dimensions for effective collaboration aforementioned provide an indication of the complexity of collaboration. Complementarity and compatibility seem to imply opposite dimensions. On the one hand, there is the added value of having different qualities in *complementarity*, on the other hand, *compatibility* suggests that being too different is not a good thing. In addition, strategies of cultural interaction for keeping the best of our own culture and adopting the best of the other, as optimal condition for developing and sustaining a collaboration, require a delicate balance of separation and blending. Plus, the temporal dynamics: over time, this balance changes (political or organizational changes, leadership changes) and need to be continuously monitored and (re-)established.

A Framework for Cultural Interoperability Assessment

We started this chapter with the following questions: What happens when organizations join a collaboration and form a new collective? What are the challenges? How to manage them to avoid the sources of failure identified in the previous section? An essential element to managing the collaboration process effectively is how the people who participate in the collaboration perceive the process and are motivated to make it work bridging differences and seeking opportunities in collaboration. It is advisable to have clear goals and objectives and to communicate them effectively, securing commitment by higher-level management involvement (*leadership from the top*) and required investment and resources to support the collaboration (*set up for success*).

The dimensions discussed above – complementarity, commitment and compatibility – provide structured anchor points for developing an assessment tool centered on human aspects of a collaboration. We linked the collaboration dimensions with 15 cultural interoperability conditions we had used in a study of strategic collaboration between Dutch and

German military units in peace time organizations (Wermser et al., 2019). Given that these military units existed already for longer times, each has developed a mix of national, military and organizational cultures. Although the context is a collaboration between two military cultures, the Dutch and Germany military cultures are different enough to require careful consideration and management efforts to develop a symbiotic culture that increases the effectiveness of the collaboration. To get deeper insight into cultural interoperability conditions we identified, below we provide details and illustrate findings of the study.

First, a short description of the setting provides a background. The context is a strategic military peace time collaboration formed in 2016 with a Dutch–German tank battalion integrated in the Dutch Mechanized Brigade *under the command* of the German 1st Panzer Division. The battalion integrates 100 Dutch and 300 German soldiers. The purpose of the collaboration was to increase synergies, including sharing of technical and operational know-how, resources, training opportunities but also using strategic motives, for both nations to build shared operational capacities. For example, for the Dutch military, that had already sold their tanks, the collaboration was an opportunity to regain access to tanks, to maintain and gain operational relevance in the international context.

The format of the collaboration, requiring deep integration with substantial control by the sourcing organizations, is interesting because this arrangement offers high potential for close collaborations at multiple – executive and execution – levels. Whereas military organizations have a hierarchical nature and structure with clear command roles, collaboration and bridging differences cannot be *ordered*. Effective collaboration is based on motivating people, building shared identity, productive interactions, concrete benefits of learning and novel capabilities. In this case, this exercise shows that even in hierarchical structures as the military, people are the central focus of operations and progress in line with Human Centered Management principles.

Note that culture can only be assessed indirectly. Asking participants questions about the characteristics and challenges of working with different cultures is in fact asking about the actual and developing manifestations of those cultures, the artifacts and behaviors of the partners. Whereas culture is a stable characteristic, learned over time and historically rooted, perceptions of the manifestations of culture may develop quickly, influenced by external conditions and shaped by partner's behaviors and purposeful interventions (Ostroff, Kinicki, & Muhammad, 2013). Assessing these perceptions allows to get a sense of the underlying cultures that provide anchor points to act upon, change conditions, develop new artifacts and promote new behaviors.

In Table 3.1, a framework with concrete conditions to assess and monitor cultural interoperability is presented. The conditions we present here aim to capture the perceptions of people in a collaboration. The

Table 3.1 Cultural Interoperability Framework

Dimensions of Effective Collaboration	Conditions of Cultural Interoperability
Complementarity	
	Organizational strategic opportunities
	Personal opportunities for learning and growing
	Pride in the collaboration
	Perceived complementarity of knowledge and skills
	Unique contribution to the collective
Compatibility	
	Extra effort
	Effectiveness of the work
	Cultural fit – interaction affinity
	Cultural fit – perceived similarity
	Cultural fit – cultural differences
Commitment	
	Means and facilities
	Motivation to collaborate
	Trust in partners
	Common identification (with partners)
	Identification with the collaboration

Source: The authors

conditions can be linked to a concrete questionnaire to address the main sources of cultural interoperability: identification with the collaboration, motivation and cultural fit. The insights from this feedback by the participants will enable leaders of collaboration to take directed action to improve collaboration processes and ensure collaboration success.

In the following sections, we explain each condition of cultural interoperability in more detail, relying on existing theory and findings from our study on cultural interoperability in a military context. For each condition, we provide an example what to ask the participants, e.g., in a survey.

Partner Complementarity Conditions

Strategic and Personal Opportunities

Understanding the strategic opportunities, and possibly necessities, for one`s organization to join a collaboration – why the collaboration is taking place – contributes to being actively involved in the collaboration. We found in our study that a majority of the respondents agreed that the collaboration offered opportunities from a strategic point of view.

Agreement was strongest for respondents who had frequent interactions with the other party. However, such positive attitudes are not a given and requires careful preparation of the collaboration.

Positively valuing organizational opportunities does not imply that the collaboration is seen as providing personal opportunities. To develop personal benefits, it is important to explicitly highlight and demonstrate the opportunities that could be explored, such as increased learning experiences (Essens & Bekkers, 2014).

Typical survey questions directly ask participants to what extent they agree that the collaboration offers opportunities for the organization and for them personally, including examples of opportunities, such as learning experiences and career opportunities.

Pride in the Collaboration

Organizational pride is a positive emotion regarding the achievements – past, present and future – of one's organization, which provides a strong source of identity with the organization (Gouthier & Rhein, 2011). In the case we studied, the collaboration was positioned as a *lighthouse project* for future collaborations and it was broadly communicated this way. The respondents, who felt high pride in the lighthouse character of the collaboration and were more engaged, were more motivated to collaborate, identified more with the collective and evaluated the collaboration more positively.

Survey questions ask about the extent to which participants agree to statements such as, *Working in this collaboration gives me the feeling to play part in something unique* or, The *creation of this collaboration is an exemplary project.*

Perceived Complementarity and Unique Contributions

Complementarity of knowledge and skills relates to the idea that the combined executional qualities of the collaboration partners will achieve better outcomes. This does not imply having more of the same, rather more diversity of knowledge and skill. Even for seemingly similar organizations, such as two military organizations, this diversity can be high. For instance, one partner may be used to have a flexible informal way of operating, while the other follows a more formal, structured approach.

The perception that collaborations partners have complementary skills and knowledge is an important positive force for motivation. However, for maximum impact, it is required that these complementary skills are actually used. More specifically, we find that participants identify more strongly and are more motivated, when they feel they are making a unique contribution to the success of the collaboration. In other words, when they feel that the complementarity skills and knowledge that they possess make a difference for the integration. In fact, participants whose unique complementary skills lay dormant feel unappreciated and eventually turn their backs on the collaboration. It can be concluded that participants who see clear complementarities between them and their collaborators and feel they make a unique contribution, identify more with the collective and are more motivated to participate.

Survey questions ask about the extent that participants agree to statements such as, "*The skills of partner A and partner B complement each other*" or, "*Partner A has know-how in areas in which partner B has less know-how*".

Partner Compatibility Conditions

Compatibility refers to the level of fit between the partners' cultures, operational structures and work routines. To capture how the people in a collaboration perceive this fit, we inquire about cultural fit directly (i.e., interaction affinity, perceived similarity and cultural differences) but also assessed levels of extra effort and perceived effectivity when collaborating, as an indirect indication of how well the cultures fit and can work together.

Cultural Fit – Interaction Affinity, Perceived Similarity and Cultural Differences

Interaction affinity refers to participants' evaluation of interactions with participants of the other nation. In our study, participants who had interactions most frequently also were most positive about this contact. In addition, participants with frequent interactions reported better learning experiences, more collaboration effectiveness, but there was no relation with extra effort (explained in more detail later). These findings about interaction affinity reflect general findings showing that interactions between groups are likely to have a positive impact on the relation between members of these groups when collaboration is required to achieve shared goals (Allport, 1954). It is the task of leaders of change to ensure that interactions are frequent and take place under the right conditions.

Perceived similarity – as manifested in similar work style, values, beliefs – with participants of the other party relates to holding more positive attitudes toward the other party, which results in easier interactions and a higher perceived effectiveness of collaboration. On the other hand, strong focus on large similarity might limit the number of potential collaboration partners and, during collaboration, create a false sense of trust. A mid level of perceived similarity might provide sufficient understanding and trust to effectively work together while maintaining a critical eye on the process of collaboration. In the present collaboration case, it was found that the similarity perception was quite diverse, with one party perceiving themselves more similar to the other party than the other way around. This emphasizes the importance of assessing perceptions of similarities rather than relying on purely factual measurements of similarity between organizations and their people. Moreover, the finding might indicate a need to sensitize employees for cultural differences as perceived by both parties.

Awareness of *cultural differences* and discussing events where these differences clearly surface is an important aspect of assigning meaning to interactions in a collaboration. Differences may be a source of conflict to be managed but can also be exploited to benefit the collective. Awareness can be developed by self-descriptions and then comparing the results and by describing unexpected behaviors and misunderstandings of the other party. The latter approach, however, has a negative framing which may hinder acceptance of the differences. Self-descriptions, how a party sees itself provides a more positive starting point for collective sensemaking. In the case at hand, stereotypes were confirmed with clear differences between the parties. The Dutch participants considered themselves high in flexibility in adapting to new situations, low on strictness in following work procedures and rules and high on directness in discussions. In contrast, the German party scored the opposite. One can easily imagine how these differences can lead to frictions. These differences need to be managed, in particular in stressful situations when time to reconsider or discuss situations is short. Choosing a particular cultural style in specific situations, by having the party with that cultural style to lead can become part of the new culture, which contributes to add value to a unique combination of qualities of the collaboration.

Survey questions ask about the extent to which participants agree to statements such as, "*The beliefs and principles of partner A are very similar to those of partner B*" or, "*The working atmosphere in partner A is like the working atmosphere in partner B*".

Extra Effort and Effectiveness of the Work

Adapting to new situations means *extra effort*. Indeed, working with participants of the other party can be more difficult given that differences of opinions are more prevalent, meaning that extra time has to be invested for mutual understanding. Relatedly, *effectiveness* can be perceived as lower when working together with the partner on daily tasks proceeds less smooth because of extra time spend on aligning cultural and structural differences. Different perceptions of time costs and effectiveness between the parties may be a source of friction. Leaders of change can offer support providing extra resources at the beginning to adjust period of a collaboration and identifying and addressing sources of extra effort upfront.

Survey questions ask about the extent participants agree with statements such as, "*It costs more effort when I work with partner A than when I work with my own people*" or, "*Due to the cooperation with partner A, I do not have enough time for my other tasks*".

Partner Commitment Conditions

Partner commitment is associated with long-term intentions of collaboration partners to invest time, effort and resources into the collaboration – the means for this have to be given by leaders of change. On an individual level, commitment reflects people's motivation to devote attention and effort to resolve obstacles and frictions, to give and build trust to partners and their identification with partners and the collaboration.

Means and Facilities

Collaborations are a new element in organizations structure and to function need to receive means and facilities. Especially at the beginning of a collaboration, means and facilities beyond what is normally required to perform tasks might be required to compensate for extra efforts mentioned above needed to bridge cultural and organizational differences. Allocating sufficient means to a collaboration is a way for leadership to signal their commitment to the collaboration. However, it is not only important that means and facilities are factually present, but also important to assess people's perceptions because leaders and participants may not always agree on what is needed and/or available. This condition also came forward in interviews with participants and in earlier studies (Essens & Bekkers, 2014). Providing fewer than promised or planned resources may be taken as a challenge to deliver that can undermine the motivation of participants and introduce friction if one party is held responsible.

Here, an open question is most adequate to allow participants to freely mention diverse aspects, triggered by a question such as, *What could be done to facilitate and/or improve cooperation with the other party?*

Motivation and Trust in Partners

Motivation refers to the personal effort employees are willing to make for the success of the collaboration. Drivers for motivation are perceived opportunities of the collaboration and the idea that one provides a unique contribution to the success of the collaboration. These relations are stronger when there are more opportunities for interaction with participants of the collaboration partner.

Trust in partners is a necessary condition to handle relational uncertainty. Trust refers to three aspects: Trust that the involved participants and their sourcing organizations deliver good intentions, have sound moral values and act according with their intentions and values (Weiss et al., 2002). Our findings show that trust was positively related to motivation, perceived similarities and perceived effectiveness but negatively related to the extra effort collaboration costs. Trust was also positively related with increased interaction, a positive sign that collaboration experiences that can feed positive expectations.

Assessing motivation and trust with partners is a good way to verify that complementarity and compatibility issues are being handled well, as high levels on these conditions generate positive complementarity and compatibility perceptions.

Survey questions ask about the extent participants agree to statements like, *I trust that my partner will do what was promised, even when we have to deal with unexpected challenges* or, *My partner does its best to help me when I have trouble doing my work.*

Common Identification and Identification with the Collaboration

People who identify with a group define themselves in terms of the group and derive self-esteem from the success and status of a group. Therefore, the goals and interest of a group become their own goals and interests (Mael & Ashforth, 1995). In a collaboration, people can identify on two different levels. Common identification refers to peoples feeling that they and people of the collaboration partner around them are part of a shared group. Thus, this identification is defined between people. This form of identification is related to motivation to collaborate and to perceptions that working together is effective.

Identification with the collaboration refers to organizational effort at large, including aspects such as the visions and goals set by leadership. Especially in larger organizations, identification with the collaboration might be harder to achieve, as the meaning of collaboration is abstract to people on the work floor. For both types of identification, we find that direct interactions, on a daily or weekly basis, is a decisive factor that enhances appreciation of the collaboration. As for motivation and trust, high levels of identification can verify that the complementarity and compatibility dimensions are handled well.

Survey questions ask about the extent to which participants agree to statements like, *The successes of our collaboration feel like my own successes* or, *I am very interested in what others think about the collaboration.*

Conclusion

The purpose of this chapter was to shed light on the often-neglected relevance of cultural interoperability as means to realize collaborations' potential for growth and innovation. The collaboration process is complex and often underfunded, leading to a strong focus on strategy at the expense of people. We introduce three dimensions for sustainable collaboration, namely complementarity, compatibility and commitment, and used these as a framework for the assessment of critical conditions of cultural interoperability. Building on a real-life example of a Dutch–German military collaboration, we illustrate the application and implementation of the framework to monitor and guide the development of cultural interoperability in interorganizational collaborations. Leaders of (future) collaborations may benefit from this framework reflecting on how to develop cultural interoperability with the intention to positioning people at the center the collaboration process.

References

Allport, G. W. (1954). *The Nature of Prejudice*. Cambridge, MA, US: Addison-Wesley.

Das, T. K., & Teng, B.-S. (2000). Instabilities of strategic alliances: An internal tensions perspective. *Organization Science*, *11*(1), 77–101.

De Vries, T., Walter, F., Van der Vegt, G., & Essens, P. (2014). Antecedents of individuals' interteam coordination: Broad functional experiences as a mixed blessing. *Academy of Management Journal*, *57*, 1334–1359.

Dhurkari, R. K., & Nandakumar, M. K. (2015). Measures of complementarity and compatibility in strategic alliances for innovation: A review of literature. *The International Technology Management Review*, *5*(4), 182–201.

Essens, P., & de Vries, T. (2016). Improving evaluation of civil-military co-operation. In G. Lucius & S. Rietjens (Eds.), *Effective Civil-Military Interaction in Peace Operations: Theory and Practice* (pp. 263–274). Berlin, Germany: Springer.

Essens, P. J. M. D., Thompson, M. T., Karrasch, A., & Jermalavičius, J. (2016). *Building effective collaboration in a comprehensive approach*, NATO report. STO-TR-HFM-227.

Essens, P. J. M. D., & Thönissen, F. H. (2015). *Common effort 2.0 - A new approach to civil-military interaction exercises: Evaluation of CE-2015* TNO report TNO 2015 R11559.

Essens, P. J. M. D., & Bekkers, F. (2014). *Cost Benefit Analysis of Strategic Cooperation: Case Study Deep Integration*. Soesterberg: TNO.

Essens, P. J. M. D., Thompson, M., Febbraro, A., Baranski, J., & Vogelaar, A. L. W. (2013). *Collaboration in a Comprehensive Approach to Operations*, NATO RTO Technical report AC/323(HFM-204).

Essens, P. J. M. D., Vogelaar, A. L. W., Tanercan, E. C., & Winslow, D. J. (Eds). (2003). *The Human in Command: Peace Support Operations*. Amsterdam: Mets & Schilt.

Gouthier, M. H. J., & Rhein, M. (2011). *Organizational Pride* and *its Positive Effects* on *Employee Behavior*. *Journal of Service Journal of Service Management*, 22, 633–649.

Gulati, R., Wohlgezogen, F., & Zhelyazkov, P. (2012). The two facets of collaboration: Cooperation and coordination in strategic alliances. *Academy of Management Annals*, 6, 531–583.

Hughes, J., & Weiss, J. (Nov. 2007). Simple rules for making alliances work. *Harvard Business Review*, *2007*, 122–132.

Kale, P., & Singh, H. (2009). Managing strategic alliances: What do we know now, and where do we go from here? *Academy of Management Perspectives*, *23*, 45–62.

Kellogg Insight (2019). *Take 5: What business leaders can learn from the military*. Retrieved from https://insight.kellogg.northwestern.edu/article/business-lessons-from-military

Lepeley, M. T. (2017). *Human Centered Management: The 5 Pillars of Organizational Quality and Global Sustainability*. Abingdon, UK: Routledge.

Mael, F., & Ashforth, E. (1995). Loyal from day one: Biodata, organizational identification, and turnover among newcomers. *Personnel Psychology*, *48*, 309–333.

Mayer, R. C., Davis, J. H., & Schoorman, F. D. (1995). An integrative model of organizational trust. *The Academy of Management Review*, *20*, 709–734.

Mitsuhashi, H., & Greve, H. R. (2009). A matching theory of alliance formation and organizational success: Complementarity and compatibility. *The Academy of Management Journal*, *52*, 975–995.

Meirovich, G. (2010). The impact of cultural similarities and differences on performance in strategic partnerships: An integrative perspective. *Journal of Management & Organization*, *16*, 127–139.

OECD. (2006). *Successful Partnerships - A Guide*. Vienna: OECD LEED Forum on Partnerships and Local Governance at Centre for Social Innovation. Accessed from www.oecd.org/cfe/leed/forum/partnerships.

Ochoa, P., Lepeley, M. T., & Essens, P. (Eds). (2019). *Wellbeing for Sustainability in the Global Workplace*. UK: Routledge.

Ostroff, C., Kinicki, A. J., & Muhammad, R. S. (2013). Organizational culture and climate. In N. W. Schmitt, S. Highhouse, & I. B. Weiner (Eds.), *Handbook of Psychology: Industrial and Organizational Psychology* (pp. 643–676). Hoboken, NJ: John Wiley & Sons Inc.

Park, S., & Ungson, G. R. (2001). Interfirm rivalry and managerial complexity: A conceptual framework of alliance failure. *Organization Science*, *12*, 37–53.

Prasanna, S. R., & Haavisto, I. (2018). Collaboration in humanitarian supply chains: an organisational culture framework. *International Journal of Production Research*, *56*, 5611–5625.

Ring, P. S., & Van de Ven, A. H. (1994). Developmental processes of cooperative interorganizational relationships. *The Academy of Management Review*, *19*, 90–118.

Sarkar, M. B., Echambadi, R., Cavusgil, S. T., & Aulakh, P. S. (2001). The influence of complementarity, compatibility, and relationship capital on alliance performance. *Journal of the Academy of Marketing Science*, *29*, 358–373.

Schein, E. H. (2009). *The Corporate Culture Survival Guide*. Warren Bennis book (New and rev. ed.) San Francisco, CA: Jossey-Bass.
Schrodt, P. (2002). The relationship between organizational identification and organizational culture: Employee perceptions of culture and identification in a retail sales organization. *Communication Studies*, *53*, 189–202.
Thanos, I. C., Papadakis, V. M. (2012). Unbundling acquisition performance: How do they perform and how can this be measured. In D. Faulkner, S. Teerikangas, & R. Joseph (Eds.). *Handbook of Mergers & Acquisitions* (pp. 114–147). Oxford: Oxford University Press.
Turiera, T., & Cros, S. (2013). *CO-Business: 50 examples of business collaboration. Infonomia*. Zero Factory S.L: Barcelona.
Wermser, F., Essens, P., & Täuber, S. (2019). *Final Report Cultural Interoperability in Project Taurus*. University of Groningen, Unpublished Internal report.
Wermser, F., Täuber, S., Essens, P., & Molleman, H. (2016). Psychological safety during military integrations. In R. Beeres, G. Bakx, E. de Waard, & S. Rietjens (Eds.), *NL ARMS Netherlands Annual Review of Military Studies 2016, Organizing for Safety and Security in Military Organizations* (pp. 147–162). The Hague: Asser Press.
Wermser, F., Täuber, S., Essens, P., & Molleman, H. (2020). *Organizational change as opportunity: Sense of continuity and functional indispensability as antecedents of collaborative identification* Manuscript submitted for publication.
Weiss, E. S., Anderson, R. M., & Lasker, R. D. (2002). Making the most of collaboration: Exploring the relationship between partnership synergy and partnership functioning. *Health Education & Behavior*, 29, 683–698.
Wood, D. J., & Gray, B. (1991). Toward a comprehensive theory of collaboration. *The Journal of Applied Behavioral Science*, 27, 139–167.

4 L-E-A-P: A New Organizational Culture Framework for Knowledge-Intensive Organizations

Vishal Gupta and Neena Gopalan

Introduction

Knowledge work refers to knowledge exploration, acquisition and exploitation that are central for developing and maintaining an organization's competitive advantage. Today's organizations are facing unprece dented uncertainties and disruptions. To be resilient and successful, organizations need to make significant efforts to inspire and sustain innovative efforts of their workforce, and especially among *knowledge workers* – employees who have to think to innovate continuously in their work. Knowledge workers have jobs across occupations, industries and sectors that need people who think proactively, among others, teachers, healthcare professionals, academics, scientists, lawyers, architects and designers.

Knowledge is the greatest leveler of our times and knowledge work is increasingly important and significant for organizations (Drucker, 1992; Wartzman, 2020). In new-age organizations driven by knowledge, the change agent is increasingly human talent, over technology, largely because technology is developed and put to use by humans. Thus, organizations need to identify and develop novel approaches to maximize the potential and wellbeing of employees. New models and frameworks have to develop and train leaders' insights to inspire, motivate and ensure wellbeing in the workplace.

Knowledge-intensive organizations understand the importance of providing a supportive culture, an important aspect often overlooked when organizations and bosses emphasize high performance at the expense of human ingenuity, creativity and responsible autonomy necessary to motivate knowledge workers.

Most organizational cultural frameworks are traditional, generic and unable to capture and explain the complex dynamics of knowledge economy cultures fast gaining global prominence. Knowledge workers, in general, have attained higher educational levels than counterparts in other professions and industries. Their sense of professionalism is contingent with work responsibility in high risk projects and uncertain environments that require a different treatment from management (Gupta, 2020; Gupta & Singh, 2015). Building upon the principles of human capital and talent management of the Human Centered Management (HCM; Lepeley, 2017), this chapter presents a new framework to capture the nuances of organizational culture in knowledge-intensive organizations.

Based on an intensive exploratory research that the first author of this study conducted at the Indian Research and Development Laboratories, we propose a novel framework of organizational culture called the L-E-A-P culture, to meet the demands of knowledge-based organizations. The acronym conveys the roles and responsibilities organizational leaders play in developing and sustaining Learning, Enjoyment, Autonomy and Performance (L-E-A-P) as the core components of this culture.

The study builds on the theoretical underpinnings of the Self-Determination theory (SDT; Deci & Ryan, 2000; Deci, Olafsen, & Ryan, 2017) and presents a human centered conceptualization of organizational culture that emphasizes L-E-A-P of knowledge workers, aligned with their wellbeing and creative performance. The theoretical arguments of SDT are linked to the management of human capital in knowledge organizations and used to develop a framework of organizational culture embedded in the ideas of HCM (Lepeley, 2017; Ochoa, Lepeley, & Essens, 2019) to write this chapter in one of the books of the Human Centered Trilogy.

The chapter is structured as follows. We describe details of the research study followed by explanation on how leadership positively influences the L-E-A-P culture by demonstrating 5 leader behaviors anchored in: task-orientation, relation-orientation, empowerment, authenticity and team building. This chapter focuses on core issues of HCM – human capital and talent management in knowledge-intensive organizations. It positions the L-E-A-P cultural framework as an enabler for building sustainable advantage over peers in a world facing the challenges of globalization and technological disruptions. The chapter also provides examples of leaders from organizations who developing L-E-A-P culture in their organizations creating positive impact on performance and the overall wellbeing of employees.

Research Study

The study was conducted in the research and development laboratories of CSIR, India's largest civilian research knowledge-intensive organization. With 38 laboratories, over 4,000 active scientists and 8,000 scientific and technical personnel, CSIR is one of the world's largest collections of industrially oriented public research laboratories and it is India's main producer of scientific and technical publications and patents.

In this study, we used in-depth qualitative interviews of 52 CSIR scientists across 5 research laboratories in the physical sciences, biological sciences, chemical sciences, material sciences and information sciences domains. Three researchers analyzed the interview transcripts coding categories and identified valuable trends. The analyses resulted in the L-E-A-P culture, described below.

L-E-A-P Culture

Findings show that knowledge workers demand a very different relationship than traditionally with the organizations where they work. To them, work is all about enabling L-E-A-P: learning (L), enjoyment (E), autonomy (A) and performance (P). When L-E-A-P components are present in balanced proportion at work, knowledge workers actually make a real leap/L-E-A-P maximizing their efforts and achieving their potential.

In contrast, if organizational focuses are only in performance without offering LEAP, then knowledge workers tend to feel constrained and stressed (Essens & Lepeley, 2019; Deci et al., 2017). Similarly, a highly challenging and low-safety environment also result in stress, while excessive safety and no challenges leads to boredom. To be successful, knowledge-based organizations need to find optimal balance between autonomy, learning and enjoyment to improve performance in the workplace (Lepeley, 2017). To achieve this balance, familiarity with the four elements of the L-E-A-P culture detailed below is helpful for organizations seeking long-term sustainability.

L – Learning

It refers to cognitive, tech and the soft skills workers acquire in the workplace, either conducting work tasks or participating in development programs and training. In congruence with the arguments of SDT (Deci & Ryan, 2000; Deci et al., 2017), learning and growth are critical for continuous improvement of knowledge workers and to a large extent, it applies to personal professional development, not to titles/positions, and tend to select employers based on personal development opportunities that are available (Gupta, 2020). Degrees and seniority no longer carry the weight they did in industrial organizations. In contrast, knowledge workers identify with communities of expertise with strategic and technical skills than those in traditional repetitive job patterns. The career paths of knowledge workers do not seek to move up hierarchical ladders and organizational structures but to move in lateral progressions within work communities and networks of expertise. They choose workplaces that provide continuous opportunities and programs to advance learning, coaching, mentoring and feedback (Lepeley, 2017).

Knowledge workers mirror themselves as learning *workers* and expect their opinions to be heard in organizational decisions concerning their career development, training and learning opportunities, using new methods and avoiding obsolete formulas unable to objectively evaluate workers' performance in knowledge organizations. This is consistent with the principle to foster quality, continuous performance, productivity improvement and excellence in organizations operating in the knowledge economy (Lepeley, 2017, 2019a, b).

E – Enjoyment: Refers to Job Satisfaction

For the most part, knowledge work is done in teams. Collaborative teams, where members recognise and assign merit to members' contributions, build trust among members contributing to enjoyable workplaces that positively affect the wellbeing of workers. Knowledge workers seek to be members of teams conducting enjoyable and stimulating tasks, and follow purposes and goals aligned with their work values and aspirations. This aspiration is in high synchrony with the principles of HCM developed for organizations functioning in the knowledge economy aiming to attain standards of quality and excellence (Lepeley, 2017).

Google, an example of knowledge company and knowledge workers, conducted a study to assess why some work team excel while others fail. A 2 years assessment, involving 180 teams with approximately 37,000 employees, was undertaken to understand what makes a perfect team (Duhigg, 2016). Results showed that teams that do well over time have a work culture characterized by *psychological safety* based on congenial conversations among members using similar amounts of time and sharing above average social sensitivity that allow all members to understand the feelings of others. Balanced active participation and sensitivity toward colleagues lead to enjoyable teamwork and higher performance.

A – Autonomy

Refers to the freedom to work according to personal interests and responsible choices to explore alternative ways to optimize efforts and attain the highest performance. The foundation of knowledge work is based on the belief that all employees have same opportunities and are equally capable to perform their job (Drucker, 1992). Knowledge workers value opportunities that allow them to assume responsibilities and be challenged to reach their optimal capacity. They prefer to do tasks that enable them to maximize the use of their talents. They shy away from work environments that force hierarchies, command and controls and bureaucratic structures (Lepeley, 2017). These workers trust in themselves to foster personal development and growth to define their own career paths and goals aligned their talents at work, life aspirations and goals. They value decision-making, value participatory management practices and expect work recognition for their efforts as well as their wellbeing beyond fair salaries. Knowledge workers tend to behave like customers expecting employers to offer them job satisfaction and a holistic *value proposition* aligned with personal and professional aspirations.

An example is that of InMobi, an India-based global provider of cloud-based intelligent mobile platforms for enterprise marketers. Recognized among innovative companies in the world, it is India's first unicorn[1] to become profitable in 2016. Work culture at InMobi is different compared to other companies, including no attendance log, employees able to take six days of leave without supervisor approval, unrestricted travel policy with little expenses reports documentation and significant trust on employees to do what is right for company. Employees are free to devote 20 percent of their time outside of their core roles on areas outside current work, enabling them to broaden prospects for lateral work opportunities. In 2014, InMobi launched a three-month bridge assessment program where employees were given the option to undertake a cross-department(s) project within the company and pick up a new skill. Once completed, an assigned mentor provided feedback. When a position within a department opened up, employees participating in bridge assignment had first preference to apply and recommended by their mentors. If any employee wanted to quit or start a new venture, the company did everything possible to support them. The company also offered free office space allowing these ex-employees to intermingle and brainstorm with ex-colleagues. The company's open-door policy offered ex-employees to be re-hired and return to InMobi (Advani, 2015; Goyal, 2015; Gupta, 2020).

P – Performance

Refers to operational activities of workers and actions conducted to fulfil the organization's mission and vision. The four components of the LEAP culture are interdependent. Therefore, performance is enhanced by learning and enjoyment is associated with autonomy leading to high performance. Echoing the core philosophy of HCM (Lepeley, 2017) argues for placing humans at the center of management and organizations in the 21st century, Naveen Tewari, Founder and CEO InMobi Group, observed that

> *The world today is far more unpredictable with many disruptive forces at work…companies today need people with very different skills to survive and flourish. They should be comfortable taking risks and thinking about disruptive ideas.*
>
> (Goyal, 2015)

Table 4.1 T-R-E-A-T Leadership Behaviors

Task-Orientation (T):	Behaviors associated with work completion optimizing talent, time and resources. Includes vision-setting, clarifying, problem-solving, monitoring, buffering behaviors. This is a necessary but not sufficient condition to ensure leaders' effectiveness as guide of knowledge workers. To excel in the knowledge work context, leaders must understand the nature of this specific kind of work and have skills to overcome work-related challenges.
Relation-orientation (R)	Behaviors aimed at creating strong interpersonal relationships in the workplace. They are based on the principle of two-way communication and by displaying these behaviors leaders facilitate, support and inspire high performance from co-workers supporting all dimension of wellbeing.
Empowering (E):	Behaviors include sharing, consulting and delegating, providing freedom and work autonomy to co-workers, making shared decisions with co-workers, inviting suggestions for work improvement, encouraging co-workers to participate incorporating ideas for innovation and continuous improvement.
Authenticity (A):	Having courage to choose what is ethical over what is easy and fast, practicing values that the leader encourages in others, setting example behavioral standards such as humility and ethics in the workplace and everywhere, showing courage and fairness to deal with co-workers ensuring trust and responsibility so that the assigned work gets completed on time regardless of unexpected impediments.
Team building (T):	Encouraging cooperation and teamwork, fostering identification with work teams, facilitating constructive conflict resolution among team members, being available to team members and emphasizing the importance of teamwork.

Source: Authors' analysis

T-R-E-A-T for L-E-A-P

Organizational leadership plays an important role influencing the L, E, and A components of work culture. Our research found that 5 core leader behavior dimensions, namely, task-orientation (T), relation-orientation (R), empowering (E), authenticity (A) and team-building (T), positively affect L-E-A-P organizational culture. We call these behavior *T-R-E-A-T leadership* and their characteristics are described in Table 4.1.

In the ensuing paragraphs, we describe how T-R-E-A-T leader behaviors can support development of L-E-A-P cultures in the workplace.

T-R-E-A-T to L-E-A-P

Knowledge work is often ambiguous and risky. Knowledge workers frequently face obstacles and challenges at work and they require and seek clarity, support, suggestions and attention from their leaders to address work-related problems. Leaders who demonstrate effective task-orientation (T), including clear vision, monitoring progress, solving problems and suggesting actions for improvement, stimulate *on-the-job learning*. Knowledge work leaders use technical competencies to evaluate and select best ideas, and lead by example to enhance employees' learning with high awareness of their wellbeing and working conditions that stimulate innovation and continuous improvement. Constantly working at improving harmony in the workplace is essential to excel at teamwork. By displaying team building behaviors, leaders can enable continuous improvement of team members through knowledge-sharing and collective learning, growth and development. Google study demonstrated that high-performing teams feel higher levels of psychological safety and are better balanced allowing all members to participate in conversations and share information in a trustful work environment without fear of disrespect or bullying (Duhigg, 2016). Trust is essential for information sharing among team members. Thus, task-orientation, leading-by-example (an aspect of Authenticity) and team-building behaviors positively influence learning (L) processes and make the L-E-A-P culture sustainable.

Employees find more intrinsic joy in their work when they feel the organization has concern for their wellbeing, when they are supported for taking work-related risks and when they believe that their jobs are valued and contributing to the fulfilment of organizational mission and goals. Leaders with relation-orientation and social skills demonstrate that they care about their employees, encourage them to support the organizational mission and vision by helping them find meaning in their work as well as develop loyalty and admiration for the organization where they work. Inspiring leaders instill a sense of pride and assist young workers understand the benefits associated with working with their organizations. Those leaders who strive for the collective's achievement are authentic in their actions, emphasize teamwork and cooperation among team members and are likely to create a psychologically safe and enjoyable workplace for their coworkers (Gupta, 2020). Thus, relation-orientation, authenticity and team-building behaviors of leaders are positively related to employees' enjoyment (E) and workplace wellbeing.

Knowledge workers usually have specialized training and expertise in their area of work. Leaders who demonstrate empowering behavior trust their co-workers and value their expertise. Knowledge workers value autonomy as a necessary condition to display their talent and creativity in innovative ways, thereby enabling higher performance and organizational productivity and competitiveness. Autonomy based on trust in the workplace gives more time to the leaders to perform other work-related activities that demand their attention. They avoid time-consuming micro-management and concentrate on organizational solutions. Figure 4.1 presents the linkages between T-R-E-A-T and L-E-A-P frameworks.

Microsoft is an example of a knowledge-intensive company where the leader has had a significant impact on organizational culture in the last years. When Satya Nadella became the CEO of Microsoft in February 2014, Microsoft had a convoluted culture of infighting, politics and inertia. Employees competed against one another to prove they were the best. The performance management system ranked employees with labels including *worst performer* in a team. Hierarchy trumpeted creativity and spontaneity (Nadella, 2017). Nadella transformed Microsoft culture first from *know-it-all* to a *learn-it-all* emphasizing that everybody can change, learn, grow and improve trying to do new things without fear of critiques of failure (Microsoft, 2020). The second change in culture Nadella initiated was to emphasize respect for others including improvement of listening skills. He distributed the book *Nonviolent Communication: A Language of Life* (Rosenberg, 2015) to all which advocates compassion and empathy as cornerstones of effective communication (Lepeley, 2017; Ochoa et al., 2019). Nadella helped his executives understand the importance of frank and fair communication, trust and understanding others rather using judgments, gossiping and nefarious criticizing. He promoted a culture of inclusiveness where workers recognize their biases but know how to manage them to avoid negative effects on other people, and where workers are able to voice their perspectives without fear of repercussions. He underlined that innovation does not happen in silos and teamwork should be enjoyable and rewarding (Nadella, 2017; Ibarra, Rattan, & Johnston, 2018). Finally, Nadella believed that the key to achieve successful culture transformation was individual empowerment and autonomy aligned with personal responsibility that allow freedom to choose to do the things workers favor. Nadella ensured that Microsoft focused on developing projects that workers enjoy doing. Company's professionals now value freedom and flexibility they cannot find in other workplaces. All these efforts led to Microsoft being ranked

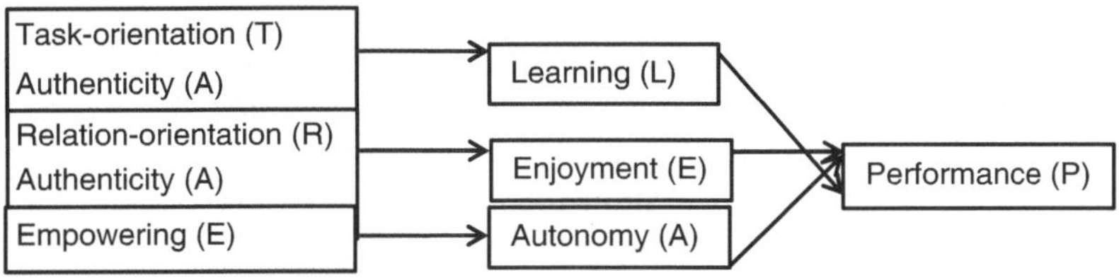

Figure 4.1 Linkages between *T-R-E-A-T* and *L-E-A-P* Frameworks.
Source: Authors' analysis.

as the 3rd most admired companies for the year 2019–2020 in the annual global ranking of Fortune magazine.[2]

L-E-A-P and Wellbeing in the Workplace

The foundations of HCM emphasize that the wellbeing of all people who work in the organization is a critical factor for active employees' commitment and work engagement that drive high performance, productivity and ultimately long-term organizational sustainability in the global VUCA (volatile, uncertain, complex, ambiguous) environment (Lepeley, 2017; Ochoa et al., 2019). In this environment, continuous external disruptions compel knowledge-intensive organizations, as much as organizations in all sectors and leaders in all industries, to pay special attention to disruptions that affect wellbeing. In this complex environment, a purely inward-looking organizational scope impairs progress. Therefore, organizations need to complement inward with an outward-looking vision effectively addressing customers' needs satisfaction and active involvement in community improvement fulfilling corporate social responsibility. In the end, the integral organizational scope determines fair competitive standards and productive capacity in inclusive organizations and societies. Stating the importance of people and the organization's philosophy of managing talent, Microsoft (2020) mentions on its website,

> *The core soul of our company, the core purpose of our company is to empower every person and every organization on the planet to achieve more. That means we want to democratize the access to technology so that you can create more technology…we all seek to unlock the unimaginable and solve the impossible.*

L-E-A-P organizational culture is focused on four essential elements: Learning (L), Enjoyment (E), Autonomy (A) and Performance (P) that our study has demonstrated to foster wellbeing among employees in knowledge-intensive companies. Our results show that when autonomy, enjoyment, learning and performance reach balanced proportion in the workplace, employees achieve an actual *leap* in wellbeing, necessary to increase their performance and job satisfaction that generates continuous productivity improvement. In contrast, when the focus is placed solely on performance, ignoring fundamental L-E-A-P elements, autonomy, learning and enjoyment, then knowledge workers feel increasingly constrained and, operations turn into a vicious spiral of deterioration for individuals' employees and the organization. Summarizing his views about cultures for knowledge-based organizations, Tewari, CEO of InMobi mentions,...

> *We are going to be a massive global internet company. We should work to remove the fear of failure. We have to create a people culture that is not just about incremental improvement but 10x [10 times earnings multiple] and truly disruptive* (Goyal, 2015).

Furthermore, Abhay Singhal cofounder of InMobi adds, We *are in the business of innovation. People – and not products and profits – are our biggest asset.* (Advani, 2015; Goyal, 2015).

Closing Statement

Until now, most motivation/organization culture theories focus on 1 or 2 variables overlooking other relevant elements necessary to secure wellbeing in the workplace critical to determine high performance. This conveys a skewed perspective that impairs long-term sustainability. Knowledge-intensive companies, where people at the center is a paradigm because all rely on human talent, are concentrated in the technology industry and consequently exposed to intense competition and continued market disruptions. Business survival is subject to high levels of resilience and agility. While all companies confront surmounting challenges in the 21st century, those such as knowledge intensive organizations are most apt to survive by engaging in deployment of the human-centered L-E-A-P culture model that can secure wellbeing to knowledge workers in this volatile global environment.

Notes

1 A unicorn is a term used in the venture capital industry to describe a privately held start-up company with a value of over $1 billion.
2 Fortune (2019). Worlds most admired companies. https://fortune.com/worlds-most-admired-companies/

References

Advani, S. (2015). *HR culture: From flexible timings to daycare, how startups are drawing policies to retain employees.* https://economictimes.indiatimes.com/small-biz/startups/hr-culture-from-flexible-timings-to-daycare-how-startups-are-drawing-policies-to-retain-employees/articleshow/48119647.cms

Deci, E. L., Olafsen, A. H., & Ryan, R. M. (2017). Self-determination theory in work organizations: The state of a science. *Annual Review of Organizational Psychology and Organizational Behavior*, *4*(1), 19–43.

Deci, E. L., & Ryan, R. M. (2000). The 'what' and 'why' of goal pursuits: Human needs and the self-determination of behavior. *Psychological inquiry*, *11*, 227–268.

Drucker, P. F. (1992). The new society of organizations. *Harvard Business Review*, *September-October*, 95–104.

Duhigg, C. (2016). *What Google Learned from Its Quest to Build the Perfect Team*. https://www.nytimes.com/2016/02/28/magazine/what-google-learned-from-its-quest-to-build-the-perfect-team.html

Essens, P., & Lepeley, M. T. (2019). *Wellbeing@work: Is buffering stress enough?* P. Ochoa, M. T. Lepeley, & P. Essens, *Wellbeing for Sustainability in the Global Workplace*. UK: Routledge.

Fortune (2019). *Worlds most admired companies*. https://fortune.com/worlds-most-admired-companies/2019/

Gupta, V. (2020). *First among Equals: TREAT Leadership for LEAP in a Knowledge-Based World*. New Delhi: Bloomsbury.

Gupta, V., & Singh, S. (2015). Leadership and creative performance behaviors in R&D laboratories: Examining the role of justice perceptions. *Journal of Leadership and Organizational Studies*, *22*(1), 21–36.

Goyal, M. (2015). Why InMobi may be India's most innovative company. https://economictimes.indiatimes.com/small-biz/startups/why-inmobi-may-be-indias-most-innovative-company/articleshow/48311479.cms?utm_source=contentofinterest&utm_medium=text&utm_campaign=cppst

Ibarra, H., Rattan, A., & Johnston, A. (2018). *Satya Nadella at Microsoft: Instilling a Growth Mindset*. US: Harvand Business Publishing (Case No.: HBP: LBS 128).

Lepeley, M. T. (2019a). *EDUCONOMY. Unleashing Wellbeing and Human Centered Sustainable Development*. US: Information Age Publishing.

Lepeley, M. T. (2019b). *EDUQUALITY. Human Centered Management in Education. A Model for Deployment, Assessment and Sustainability*. US: Information Age Publishing.

Lepeley, M. T. (2017). *Human Centered Management. The 5 Pillars of Organizational Quality and Global Sustainability*. UK: Routledge.

Microsoft (2020). Empowering our employees – Corporate Social Responsibility. https://www.microsoft.com/en-us/corporate-responsibility/empowering-employees

Nadella, S. (2017). The C in CEO stands for Culture. https://www.fastcompany.com/40457741/satya-nadella-the-c-in-ceo-stands-for-culture

Ochoa, P., Lepeley, M. T., & Essens, P. (2019). *Wellbeing for Sustainability in the Global Workplace*. UK: Routledge.

Rosenberg, M. (2015). *Nonviolent Communication: A Language of Life*. US: Puddle Dancer Press.

Wartzman, R. (2020). What Peter Drucker knew about 2020. https://hbr.org/2014/10/what-peter-drucker-knew-about-2020

5 A Social Complexity Perspective

Rehumanizing Organizational Culture with Human Centered Management for Long-Term Sustainability

Jan Willem Nuis and Pascale Peters

Narrative 1

The organizational cultural transformation program did not work out as intended. Francesca, a *classic* Human Resource manager of a mid-sized logistical firm had put in all her energy to promote *a healthy organizational culture* focused on encouraging employees to prepare and assume increasing responsibility for individual and shared decision-making to face surmounting disruptions in the work environment. With support from top management, she had developed a wide range of activities, including memos, fitness activities and mailings, aimed to entice employees across the organization to *become healthier, agile and more productive.* Additionally, all employees in the office received fresh apples with this message: Take *a bite into your own health.* To her surprise, employees were talking behind her back about such a personal health and lifestyle intervention. The deterrent effects of a healthy approach to improve the workplace induced Francesca to cancel her change program based on criticism and grievances from supervisors and the works council. What had happened?[1]

Introduction

Deep changes affecting organizations and impacting the wellbeing of people in the workplace (Ochoa, Lepeley, & Essens, 2019), including work–life balance (Kelliher et al., 2019), *the war on talent*, mismanagement of employment relationships, aging and multi-generation workforces, among others, are pressing to advance to meet the demands of the 21st century moving away from obsolete strategic human resource management (HRM) or humans-as-resources approaches and to assume responsibility for human-at-the-center of organizations, what Lepeley (2017) calls Human Centered Management (HCM).

HRM perpetuated from the industrial past guided primarily by short-term financial outcomes in many instances at the expense of employees' wellbeing and ignoring important factors that stimulate work engagement (Lepeley, 2017). In the last decades, organizations have discovered the benefits of change and are increasingly seeking *human centered approaches* required for long-term organizational sustainability and regeneration and organizational improvement centered on the wellbeing of people to advance inclusive societal capabilities (cf. Bücker Peters, & El Aghdas, 2019; Ehnert, Harry, & Zink 2014). The transformation from these traditional HRM approaches toward HCM implies that scholars and organizations need to pay more attention as to how to manage employment relationships effectively to substitute retrograde viewing of people as mere organizational resources (Janssens & Steyaert, 2009).

In her book *Human Centered Management. The 5 Pillars of Organizational Quality and Global Sustainability*, Lepeley (2017) presents basic arguments driving the paradigm shift from the mainstream but unsustainable HRM to perspectives that see human wellbeing in the workplace as a necessary condition for 21st-century organizations to attain long-term sustainability. She challenges the traditional humans-as-resources view on human employment that were instrumental in shaping Taylorian and Weberian formulas of scientific management a century ago but are no longer valid in the Knowledge and Information Age.

The human centered approach pays attention to dimensions that affect people's wellbeing and their work such as physical and mental health, employability capacity, including continuous skills and competencies upgrading and personal development and personal vitality, such as motivation, engagement and resilience. All these dimensions of employee wellbeing are necessary for individuals to develop sustainable careers in changing global labor markets (De Prins, De Vos, Van Beirendonck, & Segers, 2015) and in volatile, uncertain, complex and ambiguous (VUCA) environments (Ochoa et al., 2019).

Growing attention for these human centered approaches runs parallel with new organizational imperatives for flexibility, adaptability, agility and resilience (Lengnick-Hall, Beck, & Lengnick-Hall, 2011). They correlate highly with emerging trends focused on individuals' need for autonomy, assuming higher levels of responsibility, deeper involvement in decision-making, voice and accountability for increasingly flexible and value-based careers in the contemporary VUCA environments (Inkson, 2006). In this context, much in line with the philosophy of HCM, Ehnert, Harry, and Zink (2014) refers to the emergence of Sustainable HRM. Both Ehnert et al. (2014) and Lepeley (2017) signal a shift from a static, resource-based perspective on the employment relationship to a newly emerging human centered perspective emphasizing people's needs, values, expectations, assumptions and responsibilities that give purpose and meaning to life and work. This shift implies organizations to engage in radical *cultural* change processes that affect stakeholders' values, attitudes and behaviors across organizations and societies.

Scholars and managers alike show great interest in the subject of *organizational culture* and effective management models that enhance a new *management fashion* (Chatman & O'Reilly, 2016). In mainstream management thinking, organizational culture is often, although mostly implicitly, regarded as a concrete *object,* or something an organization *has*. This view, however, entails a rather modernistic and instrumental understanding of what organizational culture entails (Stacey, 2012). More specifically, mainstream management thinking states that *culture* is, or should be, *experienced* and *enacted* similarly by everybody who works in the organization, regardless of their position, experiences, beliefs or background. Moreover, it assumes that cultural experiences can be managed and sustained intactly over time. But it is increasingly questionable whether this notion of organizational culture is helpful to assess and promote values, attitudes and behaviors necessary to foster the HCM principles presented above.

In this chapter, we build on social complexity literature (Stacey & Mowles, 2016; Stewart, 2001) to advance the deployment of HCM discussing an alternative conceptualization of organizational culture that enables the adoption of the Human Centered Management paradigm (Lepeley, 2017). More specifically, we argue that the instrumental, static and object-like view of organizational culture, central to mainstream management literature (Chatman & O'Reilly, 2016), impairs the advancement of HCM in environments ad hoc with the hypothetical case of Francesca and her position as human resources manager.

This chapter presents an alternative aimed to rehumanize organizational culture, which here is conceptualized as a fluid *process* constantly emerging, changing and adapting. In this view, organizational culture as a process emerges out of daily, local and meaningful human interactions.

In our model, organizational culture is considered to be embedded in and often overlooked, power relationships between people. It has a dynamic character that can be a source of paradoxical tensions that need to be harnessed by organizational stakeholders (Janssens & Steyaert, 2009).

The following sections discuss the *social complexity perspective* which is central to the understanding of the micro-foundations of organizational culture as an ongoing process in organizations. It outlines key concepts of the social complexity perspective which we apply to the hypothetical case of Francesca the HR manager. The chapter concludes with a discussion of implications of the proposed alternative of a human centered *organizational culture as a process* to foster long-term sustainability for all stakeholders.

Developing a Social Complexity Theoretical Lens

Narrative 2

Bob, one of the team leaders at the logistic firm where Francesca works, was abashed when he found the apples in the pantry. To him, the apples were artifacts that resonated with previous experiences in a former job in a traditional organization where HRM was – in his opinion – patronizing and controlling, contrasting with his personal values in autonomy and independence. Furthermore, top management demanded rigorous performance improvements while he was increasingly accountable for the wellbeing of his co-workers. With his close teammate Janet, they discussed the interventions. They interacted to construct meaning to an intervention based on their past experiences with HRM and their histories interacting together sharing narratives with others.

Complex Adaptive System Thinking and Social Complexity Theory

Complexity sciences originated in the natural sciences studies on weather and climate (Chia, 1998) and the behavior of ants (Anderson & McShea, 2001). The theory of complex adaptive systems states that a complex system consists of a population of *heterogenous entities*, or *agents*, that interact based on a set of *locally* constructed dynamic rules resulting from direct interaction between agents in a particular *time-spatial context*. Even though behavior in that time-spatial context is governed by local rules, actors also have degrees of freedom to make decisions. Consequently, interaction processes between agents can be described as non-linear, on the one hand, and repetitive over time, on the other (Cilliers, 1998). This gives way for self-organizing and, in turn, shapes emergent properties of population-wide patterns of behavior as dynamic outcomes of countless local interactions in the population (Colbert & Kurucz, 2011).

It is impossible to unravel every single local interaction to understand emerging patterns of behavior in the system. However, complex adaptive systems thinking facilitates understanding how certain clear patterns of behavior emerge from seemingly chaotic interaction processes, and how subsequent actions of local agents give rise to new comprehensive properties of a particular system.

Analogously with complex adaptive systems thinking, the social complexity perspective, which is central to the understanding of organizational culture as a process leading this chapter, seeks to explain how social reality patterns of communication emerge when people interact with each other in time and space (Homan, 2016; Kira & Lifvergren,

2014; Letiche, Lissack, & Schultz, 2011; Stacey & Mowles, 2016; Stewart, 2001), and how *patterns of communication, power structures, norms and values, all emerge from the interplay of individual and group choices in local interaction* (Stacey, 2012, p. 102).

These communication patterns evolve into population-wide patterns of communication and action in a process that resonates with the concept of organizational culture. *The social complexity perspective* shows that the notion of *shared patterns of organizational behavior* considering culture as a *process* differs from the mainstream view on organizational culture that sees culture built on static proportions (Chatman & O'Reilly, 2016). The next section discusses how organizational culture is conceptualized from a social complexity perspective emphasizing the core concepts.

Organizational Culture and the Social Complexity Perspective

Patterns of Communication and Power Relationships

The social complexity perspective focuses on the *micro-foundations* of organizational culture and *interactions* between people. It assumes that people are inherently social beings that interact with others and are consciously or unconsciously reflexive. When a person interacts with others, *expectations* about others influence the person's attitudes and behaviors consciously and unconsciously. In the process, the person conducts self-assessment as an object estimating an outcome or responses received from other people, including all the people involved in the interaction and also including previous human interactions, both within and outside the organization.

When people communicate, they exchange gestures (written, spoken language and non-verbal symbols), which are interpreted and responded to by others in a reflexive interaction process. However, the intentions behind gestures can be interpreted in multiple expected but also unexpected ways. This process, in turn, generates a wide range of responses from those involved in the interaction. In this process of mutual exchange of gestures and responses among people, coined *turn-taking*, new patterns of narratives emerge that may explain new meanings that emerge from social interaction and associated outcomes. Such new patterns can give future social interactions a sense of normality, reflecting the *normal* way to discuss things within a specific context (Stacey & Mowles, 2016).

Narrative 3

Bob considers the apples a patronizing gesture from the HRM department, in a context that is clearly outside of his direct time-spatial context and where different meanings have emerged. Irritated, he discusses the issue with his teammate Janet. To invigorate his arguments and to influence Janet, he refers to his previous experiences. Doing so, he intends to put her in her place by emphasizing her perspective based on their earlier interactions. Since Janet had heard about these experiences before, she responds by agreeing with Bob. She confirms his view with personal anecdotes on experiences she felt that were paternalistic in nature. In repeated interactions, Bob and Janet interpret the apple gesture assigning a meaning to Francesca's policy as *patronizing* and *anti-autonomy*, even though they had never met Francesca in person. Hence, in this case, it is not the apples as such, but what the apple represents and where it comes from (HRM), can be considered the *real* problem. With this outcome, Bob and Janet have confirmed how important autonomy is to them.

Inevitable social interactions are affected by power differences that enable or constrain the behavior of human beings (Griffin & Stacey, 2006). More importantly, people tend to ascribe more power to people who have more access to valuable resources including decision-making autonomy, time, money, knowledge, networks and authority (Elias & Scotson, 1994). When confronted with spontaneous situations and emerging realities, people try to influence others to support their experiences building on experiences they gained in previous interactions. Through interactive social processes, people assign meaning to social experiences labeling them and using individual power to try to convince others about the validity of their viewpoints (Stacey & Mowles, 2016). In other words, power differences help shape the narratives that emerge out of local interaction.

Narrative 4

The discussion between Bob and Janet is not neutral. Janet is listening to Bob, who is her team leader, while anticipating his reactions. Bob has the highest position in the team and his opinion matters. Moreover, her upbringing and education taught her that she should always value the superior's opinion. Another team member, Edward, joins the conversation. In contrast to Bob, he is enthusiastic about the apples. He thinks this is a nice gesture that also addresses important questions on health that impact the wellbeing in the workplace. He tries to contribute to the discussion but decides to step down because he feels ignored with divergent opinions creating a social distance he would rather avoid. Also, other team members join the discussion, and, because of the power dynamic, they start to share Bob's viewpoint of the apples and what it symbolizes; in spite of the fact that they had not read the memo nor seen the apples.

Generalization and Idealization

When people engage in social local interactions, they tend to generalize themes that emerge in a particular context and start sharing them as *the normal*. This new theme becomes a *social object* or a *generalized tendency for a large number of people who start acting alike in similar situations* (Griffin & Stacey, 2006, p. 16). This *social object* is intangible not affected by or has properties beyond daily human experience. Interestingly, people tend to idealize *social objects* and imagine and treat them *as if* they have overriding motives or entrenched values (Stacey & Mowles, 2016). When more people idealize these generalizations, they become *cult values*, or *an idealized future state*. This can be viewed as an imagined construct that serves as guide to gain followers. Together with power dynamics, cult values shape the organizational ideology as *a form of social communication that preserves the current order and makes it seem natural* (Stacey, 2003, p. 125).

> **Narrative 5**
> The interactions between Bob, Janet and other team members lead to a generalized discussion about the proposed intervention about the apples concluding they symbolize an intrusion in their autonomy. If the organization wants to promote employees' wellbeing, they should think about autonomy, not apples! To them, autonomy is a social object. When their discussion continues, they increasingly idealize autonomy as the most important value applicable in all situations, concluding that the organization should focus on autonomy rather than giving away apples. Autonomy turns into a cult value in the context of this team.

Evaluation and Particularization

Social interactions are always subject to evaluation. People choose their actions, commonly unconsciously, based on personal intentions, desires and values and past history of social interaction and social objects. When people discuss how they perceive gestures, they are simultaneously re-interpreting previous interactions on the same topic and adapt them to a particular time-spatial context. Inferring that cult values provide generalizations about what *the person should pursue* and how these cult values are adapted to the prevailing time-spatial context (i.e., particularization) over and over again (Stacey, 2012). Hence, human interaction generates unintended consequences that affect behaviors when interpretations of cult values are reproduced in a context but are also replaced by new interpretations.

The above-discussed process of evaluation explained why the intentions of management, for instance, in strategic organizational policies and practices, in the same organization can be interpreted in different contexts in different ways (Wright & Nishii, 2013).

Narrative 6

Bob and Janet have discussed with other team members *the apples-intervention* referring to previous experiences they have had. They also interpret the intervention in light of their local praxis and history. This implies that the apple and what it symbolizes to them is evaluated to fit their locally constructed reality. While Francesca tried to impose the cult value of *healthy lifestyles* according to the HRM department on the local team members, in the discourse of this team, *autonomy* is an important value. Consequently, the memo and interventions from HRM are evaluated against a specific *backdrop* that deviates from what they consciously experience as normal.

Connectedness

The *cult values* shared by people in interactions are often shared with others beyond the local context and beyond organizational boundaries. Consequently, *social objects,* and particularly *cult values,* are copied through interpretations of other people that may result in organization-wide value-based narratives resembling an organizational culture. This explains how local cult values that connect people (connectedness) be adopted across boundaries and may be adapted to fit local narratives (Kira & Van Eijnatten, 2008). This idea implies that social interactions can reproduce elements of the previous organizational culture and introduce new elements to the organizational culture. This explains how close social interactions and understanding of local and organizational social object, cult values and discourses are key elements for organizational stakeholders to be able to transform and rehumanize organizational culture, that is, to replace the obsolete humans-as-resources management approaches by HCM (Lepeley, 2017).

Narrative 7

Bob is well connected in the organization to team managers and other workers. In informal meetings, he shares his ideas about autonomy, dispersing this cult value. His tenure and character make him convincing for colleagues to sympathize with his narrative on autonomy and an apparent lack of autonomy in the organization. Other team leaders adopt his ideas and, in turn, discuss them with their teams. In this process, they make them fit within respective local contexts. Thus, the discourse on the cult value of autonomy spreads, as positively evaluated and particularized. Over time, it then seems normal to reject the apples-initiative. The value of autonomy, although it has many different interpretations, has become part of the organization-wide narrative among people, making it normal in the particular time-spatial context.

Formulating Human Centered Organizational Culture

As Lepeley makes clear when she spells the foundations of HCM (2017), it is necessary to replace obsolete human-as-resource approaches inherited from the industrial past with new agile ones that position the wellbeing of people at the center of organizational culture and the sustainability purpose. This implies redefining management imperatives focused on resources and adopting innovative approaches that create value for the organization highly aligned with the wellbeing of employees, customers and society at large. Culture is embedded in intrinsic social relationships where people interact with other people, so the static perspective of organizational culture is no longer effective in the new social workplace. The social complexity perspective offers a conceptual perspective of organizational culture aligned with new insights for HCM practice.

Narrative 8

Francesca has heard that her program is ridiculed and overshadowed by a topic of autonomy mentioned a lot. People complain that a lack of autonomy is affecting their wellbeing. Frustrated Francesca seeks expert advice from Dolores, an experienced transformational manager with a clear human centered approach to organizational culture. Dolores encourages Francesca *to get out of her office* and start asking people what really helps them achieve wellbeing. Dolores, aware that people always *define their own reality* recommends Francesca that she should be present to better understand the local discourse on wellbeing and health, organizational values and specific needs. She also introduces values such as participation, respect, openness, employee voice and dialogue that are critical to understand the organizational culture. According to Dolores, it is impossible to design, engineer or implement a culture based purely on the complex result of countless interactions. She stresses that Francesca really has to observe thoroughly to understand and co-create dialogues with others. *Don't assume you know what is going on but learn what is going on.* Interact to co-create shared values! Francesca learns that efforts to transform a culture start by changing her behavior and the way she talks about the culture and to get involved in an open discussion with other people in the organizations to become familiar with their needs and expectations, showing and sharing human centered values and the explicit model she is promoting to meet their values and needs to enhance wellbeing in the workplace.

Organizational Culture as a Process

Successful deployment of HCM requires to substitute static industrial perspective of organizational culture to advance transformation into resilient, agile and innovative perspectives centered on wellbeing as the focus of organizational culture. The transformation implies that ideas and values about organizational culture needs to be *dynamized*, rehumanized and refocused on social interaction that are essential to attain wellbeing.

It has been discussed across the chapter that organizational culture is often described as a *thing* that is, or ought to be, experienced similarly by all people in the organization, regardless of previous experiences and other effects. Additionally, organizational culture may be assessed as *agile*, *healthy* or *people-oriented*. Conversely, from the social complexity perspective, organizational culture is a social phenomenon and an outcome of dynamic interactions between people over time that results in a myriad of interactions within and across teams and also outside the organization. Social interactions lead to new patterns of communication between people on a daily basis when they negotiate, acquire and convey new meanings. Organizational culture is shaped and communicated in narratives and language of social interactions as organizational processes (Wittmayer et al., 2019). Social interactions create *imaginative dimensions* (i.e., social objects and cult values) that can only *exist* where people interact and participate in social contexts that are inherently illusive not as material possessions, or something an organization *has* but describes what it *is*. When organizational culture is described, it is generalized, often idealized and adapted to new interactions with high potential to lead to recurrent and stable behavioral patterns. But cultures are fluid and always in motion transferred and altered through emerging narratives (Stacey, 2012).

Participation and Voice

The organizational culture associated with HCM is deployed in flat, matrix and non-hierarchical organizational structures built on the wellbeing of people as a precondition to reach high performance and productivity that are essential to attain long-term organizational sustainability. Organizational culture shaped on HCM is built on active participation and voice of all the people who work in the organization, valuing and stimulating individual talents, cognitive, hard and Soft Skills and workers' engagement and motivation with high awareness that wellbeing depends on physical and mental health, empathetic and social interactions, the satisfaction of economic and financial needs and community participation that altogether determine life purpose and enhance work commitment. Organizational culture aligned with HCM is shaped by daily experiences, narratives and collective efforts of people who work in the organization regardless of position, tenure or type of employment contract (Lepeley, 2017, Ochoa et al., 2019). Active employees' participation, co-creation (Metz et al., 2019) and dialogue are critical for high performance built on collaboration and people's continuous commitment to engage in independent and in collective projects aimed at meeting organizational goals with tasks at hand (Klein, Cooper, Molloy, & Swanson, 2014).

Practical Implications

The chapter's discussion has clarified that organizational culture is difficult to identify and measure. This statement is not intended to dissuade human centered practitioners and advisors from their responsibility to promote human centered organizations and sustainability. On the contrary, the social complexity perspective offers theoretical and practical transformational strategies to be deployed in contingency with the following requirements: first, social complexity is embedded in social interactions; therefore, HC practitioners need to immerse in the organization to be transformed aiming to understand critical aspects of OC that require deep involvement (Elias, 1987) and ample engagement across the organizations, and this means from top management literally to the cleaning personnel. To get to know the organizational culture, practitioners have to dive deep into the local environment connecting with social realities across the workplace analyzing how people deal with structural and functional elements. This kind of involvement requires progress from observation into action and from detached inspection to active participation, and creation of social organizational interactions necessary to grasp meanings and patterns of influence. Second, the narrative nature used to facilitate social complexity analysis requires practitioners with Soft Skills that are essential to facilitate inclusive and pluralist *dialogues* (Ackers, 2019) within and between groups of people across the organization and especially Soft Skills needed to manage ambiguity and coping with paradoxes inherent in spontaneous social interactions. Third, because power structure is important in social complexity, practitioners responsible for people management in human centered organizations must learn to sense and subtle influence *power dynamics* (Elias & Scotson, 1994). Finally, because conceptions on human centered culture HCM need to de-instrumentalized HRM approaches, people in the organization must be able to evaluate *practical judgments* about social interactions leading to actions (phronesis) to influence the transformation (Stacey, 2012) and deployment of Human Centered Organizatioal Culture.

Note

1 The narratives included in this chapter aim to illustrate in practice the application of a theoretical model to advance the deployment of the Human Centered Organizational Culture. The analysis starts at the micro-level of interaction and expands to organization-wide narratives.

References

Ackers, P. (2019). Neo-pluralism as a research approach in contemporary employment relations and HRM: Complexity and dialogue. In K. Townsend (Ed.), *Elgar Introduction to Theories of Human Resources and Employment Relations* (pp. 34–52). US: Edward Elgar Publishing.

Anderson, C., & McShea, D. W. (2001). Individual versus social complexity, with particular reference to ant colonies. *Biological Reviews*, *76*(2), 211–237.

Bücker, J., Peters, P., & El Aghdas, N. (2019). Managing the future workforce in a sustainable way: Exploring paradoxical tensions associated with flexible work. In A. Lopez-Cabrales & R. Valle-Cabrera (Eds.), *Human Resource Management at the Crossroads: Challenges and Future Directions* (pp. 160–188). UK: Cambridge Scholars Publishing.

Chatman, J. A., & O'Reilly, C. A. (2016). Paradigm lost: Reinvigorating the study of organizational culture. *Research in Organizational Behavior*, *36*, 199–224.

Chia, R. (1998). From complexity science to complex thinking: Organization as simple location. *Organization*, *5*(3), 341–369.

Cilliers, P. (1998). *Complexity and Postmodernism: Understanding Complex Systems*. US: Psychology Press.

Colbert, B. A., & Kurucz, E. C. (2011). A complexity perspective on strategic human resource management. In P. Allen, S. Maguire, & B. McKelvey (Eds.), *The SAGE Handbook of Complexity and Management*. US: SAGE Publications.

De Prins, P., De Vos, A., Van Beirendonck, L., & Segers, J. (2015). Sustainable HRM for sustainable careers: Introducing the 'Respect Openness Continuity (ROC) model.' In A. De Vos & B. I. J. M. Van Der Heijden (Eds.) *Handbook of Research on Sustainable Careers* (pp. 319–334). US: Edward Elgar Publishing.

Ehnert, I., Harry, W., & Zink, K. J. (Eds.). (2014). *Sustainability and Human Resource Management*. Berlin: Springer.

Elias, N. (1987). *Involvement and Detachment*. UK: Blackwell.

Elias, N., & Scotson, J. L. (1994). *The Established and the Outsiders* (Vol. 32). US: SAGE.

Griffin, D., & Stacey, R. (2006). *A Complexity Perspective on Researching Organisations: Taking experience seriously*. US and Canada: Routledge.

Homan, T. (2016). Locating complex responsive process research in the approaches of theorising about organisations. *International Journal of Business and Globalisation*, *17*(4), 491–513.

Inkson, K. (2006). Protean and boundaryless careers as metaphors. *Journal of Vocational Behavior*, *69*(1), 48–63.

Janssens, M., & Steyaert, C. (2009). HRM and performance: A plea for reflexivity in HRM studies. *Journal of Management Studies*, *46*(1), 143–155.

Kelliher, C., Richardson, J., & Boiarintseva, G. (2019). All of work? All of life? Reconceptualising work-life balance for the 21st century. *Human Resource Management Journal*, *29*(2), 97–112.

Kira, M., & Lifvergren, S. (2014). Sowing seeds for sustainability in work systems. In I. Ehnert, H. Wes, & K. J. Zink (Eds.). *Sustainability and Human Resource Management* (pp. 57–81). US: Springer.

Kira, M., & Van Eijnatten, F. M. (2008). Socially sustainable work organizations: A chaordic systems approach. *Systems Research and Behavioral Science*, *25*(6), 743–756.

Klein, H. J., Cooper, J. T., Molloy, J. C., & Swanson, J. A. (2014). The assessment of commitment: Advantages of a unidimensional, target-free approach. *Journal of Applied Psychology*, *99*(2), 222.

Lepeley, M. T. (2017). *Human Centered Management: 5 Pillars of Organizational Quality and Global Sustainability*. UK: Routledge.

Lengnick-Hall, C. A., Beck, T. E., & Lengnick-Hall, M. L. (2011). Developing a capacity for organizational resilience through strategic human resource management. *International Human Resource Management: Theoretical and Strategic Advances*, *21*(3), 243–255.

Letiche, H., Lissack, M., & Schultz, R. (2011). *Coherence in the midst of complexity: Advances in social complexity theory*. US: Springer.

Metz, A., Boaz, A., & Robert, G. (2019). Co-creative approaches to knowledge production: What next for bridging the research to practice gap? *Evidence & Policy: A Journal of Research, Debate and Practice*, *15*(3), 331–337.

Ochoa, P., Lepeley, M. T., Essens, P. (2019). *Wellbeing for Sustainability in the Global Workplace*. UK: Routledge.

Stacey, R. (2003). *Complexity and group processes: A radically social understanding of individuals*. UK: Routledge.

Stacey, R. (2012). *Tool and Techniques of Leadership and Management: Meeting the Challenge of Complexity*. UK: Routledge.

Stacey, R., & Mowles, C. (2016). *Strategic Management and Organisational Dynamics. The Challenge of Complexity to Ways of Thinking about Organisa tions*. (7th ed.). UK: Pearson Education.

Stewart, P. (2001). Complexity theories, social theory, and the question of social complexity. *Philosophy of the Social Sciences*, *31*(3), 323–360.

Wittmayer, J. M., Backhaus, J., Avelino, F., Pel, B., Strasser, T., Kunze, I., & Zuijderwijk, L. (2019). Narratives of change: How social innovation initiatives construct societal transformation. *Futures*, *112*, 102433.

Wright, P., & Nishii, L. (2013). Strategic HRM and organizational behavior: Integrating multiple levels of analysis. In J. Paauwe, D. Guest, & P. Wright (Eds.), *HRM and performance: Achievements and challenges*. US: John Wiley & Sons.

6 Virtuous Human Centered Organizational Culture

The Case of People with Disabilities

Armand Bam and Linda Ronnie

Introduction

All-embracing communities where humanity, empathy and compassion for all people foster inclusion and value diversity are at the heart of Human Centered Management (HCM) (Lepeley, 2017). Nonetheless, the case of people with disabilities (PWD) related to work is under-researched in management and organizational culture in spite of the evidence that work is a crucial factor in personal development and effective participation in multiple social roles (Holmqvist, 2009).

In effect, PWD confront recurrent difficulties in corporate communities and very restrictive work opportunities compared to most people. Although the practice of exclusion of PWD is not new and has a tradition, new knowledge of human development and the benefit associated with inclusiveness in organizations and societies worldwide deserves special attention as essential values and morals to build a human centered culture in organizations.

Legislation plays a vital role in eliminating discriminatory and unfair employment practices. But deep reliance on laws tend to obscure and overlook the benefits of inclusive and holistic practices, as opposed to legitimate human practices to advance organizational theories (Thomas, 2003). In the last decade, increasing numbers of organizations are embracing local and international initiatives to promote inclusiveness through rights-based approaches to meet legislative imperatives (Araten-Bergman, 2016). But instead of successful outcomes, a declining number of PWD in meaningful employment worldwide (Kalef, Barrera, & Heymann, 2014) demonstrates that the approach is flawed and not meeting expectations.

Aristotelian virtue ethics, as a dynamic theory of business, offer a comprehensive ethical vision able to ensure the development and advance of human centered organizations and inclusive practices (Arjoon, 2000). This theory asserts that, in order to become sustainable in the global VUCA (volatile, uncertain, complex, ambiguous) environment of the 21st century, organizations need to adopt and deploy ethical principles such as Universal Design (UD) to promote the inclusion of PWD

(Barclay, Markel, & Yugo, 2012). This chapter discusses how organizations address and promote the development of a human centered and inclusive organizational culture for all employees using virtuous practices to consolidate this vision.

The New Value of Virtues in Business

In the 21st century, workplace diversity and inclusion are not only increasingly regarded as ethical imperatives, but also add a significant dimension to competitive advantages of organizations in general and businesses in particular. Most recently, management discourses have focused on values as one of the most important driving forces for ethical behavior in organizations of all sectors and worldwide.

In this case, values are described as core beliefs and thoughts leaders utilize as a moral compass to make decisions. This notion of values contrasts with virtues reflecting personal characteristics that uphold moral excellence. Whereas virtues are practiced continuously, values are considered guiding principles aimed at achieving personal and social objectives.

In terms of workplace diversity, values-based actions such as prioritizing good practice codes and meeting inclusiveness targets have not fulfilled expectations as employment rates of PWD continue declining. Amidst the present shortcomings of values-based approaches, alternatives solutions are required. By the same token, the application of a virtue framework that upholds continuous pursuit and integrated moral imperatives of people and the community presents a promising methodology for increasing inclusion of PWD in business organizations.

Virtuous organizations are built on the purpose that ethics implies not only to acknowledge what is good but also to work continuously on the pursuit of doing good things that contribute to improve the wellbeing of all people in the *polis* [community]. Virtuous people drive virtuous organizations promoting that doing the right thing depends on people and the organizational context over and above the mere application of a law.

McIntyre's work has been instrumental in furthering inquiry into ethical leadership and organizational behavior. In *After Virtue,* he presents a broad historical critique of modernity and the erosion of virtues in societies and business organizations. At the heart of his critique, he and Lepeley identify hierarchical bureaucratic resource focused management of the industrial past as a critical shortcoming of modern work and human centered organizations (MacIntyre, 2007, Lepeley, 2017, Ochoa, Lepeley, & Essens, 2019, Lepeley, Kuschel, Beutell, Pouw, & Eijdenberg, 2020), and so do Majluf and Abarca in their book Human Centered Leadership, which is part of this Human Centered Management Book Trilogy.

MacIntyre assesses virtues in business distinguishing between practice and institution. Practice is considered a human activity that creates meaning and inspires individuals to transform their environments in pursuit of improved personal wellbeing and collective benefits. Understanding the meaning of practice helps professionals evaluate what living a virtuous life means. Through a resurgence in societal demand for increasing responsibility and morality in organizations, businesses and management are called to play a central role in restructuring work environments providing optimal conditions where employees are invited to continuously engage in virtuous practice at work and in life.

Virtuous Practice and Inclusion

The Aristotelian approach applied to business implies living a good life aiming to achieve *eudemonia,* finding life purpose as a responsibility for continuous self-improvement as a necessary condition to help others optimizing human connectedness as a critical dimension of long-term wellbeing (Solomon, 1992, Lepeley, 2017, Ochoa et al., 2019, Lepeley et al., 2020).

In HCM, living a good life is about the pursuit of continued self-improvement to attain sustainable wellbeing while supporting others to achieve the same in work and life (Lepeley, 2017). Similarly, for Aristotelian *eudemonia*, wellbeing is a long-term endeavor (Bam & Ronnie, 2020). Virtues are practiced with the dual purpose of nurturing individual wellness and serving the common good of the community and businesses that provide services. HCM based on fundamental economic principles is anchored in ethics, moral values, freedom and eudemonic personal responsibility to advance self and to continuously improve institutions and society (Lepeley, 2017, Lepeley, 2019a, 2019b).

Proponents of virtue ethics suggest that organization managers have the intrinsic moral duty of contributing to building their communities beyond ensuring the profitability of a company. In fact, Corporate Social Responsibility (CSR) practiced by growing numbers of modern organizations shows that businesses increase profits when leaders adopt ethically motivated strategies adding an outward-looking dimension for improvement reaching the communities where customers come from over the traditional inward scope of compliance strategies.

In ethical-based workplaces, diversity and inclusion are embedded in the organizational culture and recognized as a common practice leading to continuously increasing wellbeing of all the persons who work in the organizations to stimulate work commitment and engagement leading to higher organizational performance.

HCM promotes development and strengthening of virtuous organizational culture that prioritizes human interactions and collaborative actions as instrumental efforts for moral flourishing and fostering mutual understanding that is essential to deter and eliminate prejudice and conflict between individuals and teams in modern organizations

(Lepeley, 2017). Business organizations that are all-embracing communities are those where humans are at the center and compassion for others supports diversity. Part of the moral task of managers is promoting participation of PWDs to help them become productive members of the working community that can contribute their special talents in virtuous culture of inclusion that seek the wellbeing of all members of HC organizations in inclusive societies.

Universal Design

According to the Centre for Excellence in Universal Design (2020), UD is the design and development of an environment accessible and used by all people regardless of their age, size, ability or disability. UD is consistent with a virtue theory approach with the purpose to advance organizational culture from accommodation and inclusion into effective action (Barclay et al., 2012). UD exists in the workplace but has received less attention in comparison to the need for specialized accommodation of PWDs.

An effective UD culture promotes access and full engagement to all citizens through continuous efforts reorienting priorities and active conversations of theories (Dolmage, 2017, p. 118). UD provides PWD opportunity to experience agency and autonomy focusing on their contributions to build inclusive communities. Organizations deploying the UD culture reduce focus on accommodation of PWD because they consider the needs of all people to consolidate a barrier-free workplace. UD is an instrumental strategy to advance support for PWD in the workplace creating accessible venues for their presence and active participation. The principles of UD are summarized in Table 6.1.

Putting Aristotelian Ethics to Work for PWD

Many of the current frameworks designed to assist managers creating diverse and inclusive organizations undermine the ethos of inclusion with top-down approaches. In response, this chapter proposes a holistic framework built in the human centered ethos of UD to enhance the experiences of PWD in organizational cultures practicing and promoting Aristotelian virtues. The framework addresses three levels of work in organizations: pre-employment phase, employment phase and developing an inclusive organizational culture.

Pre-Employment Phase

Readiness to Seek Employment

PWD's readiness to seek employment is influenced by previous experiences seeking employment, with rehabilitation agencies and periods of

Table 6.1 Principles of Universal Design

Principle 1: Equitable use	• UD is applicable to people with a multiple range of abilities • Use of the design is easy to understand, regardless of user’s experience, knowledge, language skills or concentration level
Principle 2: Flexibility in use	• UD accommodates a wide range of individual preferences and abilities • Provides choice of methods
Principle 3: Simple and intuitive use	• UD is easy to understand, regardless of user's experience, knowledge, language skills and current concentration levels • Eliminates unnecessary complexity
Principle 4: Perceptible information	• UD communicates information to help all users regardless of ambient conditions or sensory abilities
Principle 5: Tolerance for error	• The design minimizes hazards and adverse consequences of accidental or unintended actions

(*Continued*)

Table 6.1 (Continued)

	• Provides safe features
Principle 6: Low physical effort	• The design is used efficiently and comfortably with minimum fatigue • Minimizes sustained physical effort
Principle 7: Size and space for approach and use	• Appropriate size and space are provided for approach, reach, manipulation and use, regardless of user's body size, posture or mobility. • Provides adequate space for the use of assistive devices

Source: Adapted from Mace (1997, p. 1)

introspection. Previous experiences influence how willing PWD are to seek employment. Continual experiences of rejection increase self-doubt and tend to prolonged periods of unemployment. Rehabilitation agencies can assist PWD to seek employment. Our framework encourages agencies to play an effective role providing necessary physical and emotional support to PWD. Studies show that business organizations can learn and benefit from the support of rehabilitation agencies (Buys & Rennie, 2001; Kulkarni & Kote, 2014). Virtuous organizations have well-developed relationships with rehabilitation agencies as part of their CSR to help community improvement that facilitate recruitment of PWD. From an Aristotelian perspective, empathy, friendliness and appreciation of diversity are required to achieve these objectives. Moore (2005) described virtuous managers as flexible and agile in their approach, as shown in UD Principle 2. They recognize that these agencies are an important resource to provide more effective support to PWD as current and prospective employees.

HC managers understand the impact of past experiences of exclusion on PWD's readiness and know how to correct to effectively manage their future prospects. PWD can easily have negative perceptions regarding how other people perceive them. These perceptions are often not tested but are assumed based on personal experiences with discrimination. Managers are aware that, despite employment opportunities, PWD need to transform negative into positive perceptions in order to access and optimize work opportunities. Human centered organizations play a key role in transforming perceptions aimed at increasing access of PWD as an important component of their culture and institutional profile.

Access to Employment

Access to employment for PWD is influenced by legislation, organizational culture and networks (Bam & Ronnie, 2018). Legislation, like the Disabilities Discrimination Act in the UK focused on eliminating employment gaps, has proven ineffective in the long term (Pope & Bambra, 2005). Legislative approaches also have unexpected consequences hindering UD in organizational compliance cultures that fail to adopt policies that by nature are simple and intuitive, as shown in UD Principle 3.

Our experience shows that policy-driven approaches alone cannot achieve meaningful employment opportunities for PWD. Instead, a virtuous organizational culture communicated through recruitment advertising to attract PWD is more likely to create access to employment. Virtuous organizations that include PWD foster diversity and are consistent with Aristotelian virtues of opportunity for all and inclusiveness also provide access to learning and educational opportunities (Barclay et al., 2012). Therefore, communications during the recruitment phase, from advertising to interviews, need to unequivocally convey the organization's commitment to inclusiveness and accessibility to people with diverse kinds of abilities (UD Principle 1).

Environmental Barriers

Employment access and opportunities may be practical constrained by institutional barriers in the work environment embedded in organizational structures, policies and attitudes (Bam & Ronnie, 2018). There are additional physical barriers that obstruct employment opportunities for PWD and must be properly addressed to provide realistic and effective hiring programs (McFarlin, Song, & Sonntag, 1991). Environmental and physical barriers are important impairments on personal hiring and functioning for PWD that organizations must understand and accommodate. Overall, all organizations need high awareness of the fact that although environments may change, impairments will remain unless corrected. Organizations that draw on the Aristotelian virtue of empathy to display compassion and attentiveness show significantly better outcomes (Shanahan & Hyman, 2003).

Deep understanding of personal barriers allows virtuous organizations to focus on removing environmental barriers that create discomfort or difficulty for PWD in the workplace. Strategies such as providing transport for disable employees or flexible work-from-home transportation arrangements, shown in UD Principles 2 and 6, may advance this goal.

Pain management is another consideration as a structural barrier in the workplace, considering that prolonged periods of pain limit people's ability to perform effectively and cause potential risk of further injury. Attentiveness and compassion of managers including coworkers help to build a caring culture where employees communicate their needs, while resilient and agile policies make it possible for PWD to participate in the workplace and make contributions to business and organizations in all sectors aiming to advance inclusive and sustainable societies worldwide.

The Employment Phase

Induction Processes

Organizations must start discussions about disability-related specific needs at the earliest point of the working relationship. Induction and orientation processes should include and clearly establish the organizational culture focused on virtue of trust (Solomon, 1999). To avoid adverse consequences and reduce potential hazards identified in UD Principle 5, induction processes need to provide PWD opportunity to engage in and establish dialogue with managers regarding their needs and most importantly with coworkers just becoming aware of PWD in the workplace. Managers must use induction as an opportunity to create open dialogue about needs to educate other people instead of deferring this responsibility to external experts on PWD who may help to facilitate the process. When this process is effectively conducted, it leads to higher levels of integration and organizational inclusion for PWD over the long term (Bam & Ronnie, 2018). Special consideration must be given during induction periods to critically influencing the attitudes and behaviors of other employees regarding inclusion and successful UD for PWD.

In most organizations, the virtue of graciousness in organizational cultures (Solomon, 1999) is impaired when managers maintain excessive control over all aspects of the induction process. Our framework proposes that PWD, who usually provide minimal input and have no participation in decision-making, should be invited to take part in induction processes to improve the narratives that expedite decisions and actions (Schur, Kruse, & Blasi, 2009). Managers' virtue of temperance can avoid self-indulgent and enhance collaborative approaches (Aristotle, 1955).

Disability Disclosure

Disclosure of disability is influenced by personal control, consent, manager influence, timing and responses from others. PWD need to pay attention and have as much control as possible about when and how their disabilities are communicated in the organization (Bam & Ronnie, 2020). Studies have addressed disclosure from an avoidance of bias and stigmatization approach (Robert & Harlan, 2006). However, PWD, as owners of their personal experiences, should have the option to prefer whether to disclose disability or not.

Markel and Barclay (2009) showed that early disclosure may be beneficial to PWD as they might be perceived as more qualified. If PWD choose to disclose, it is best to do so during the recruitment, selection and induction processes. Personal disclosure in intimate circumstances would be more effective than in open forums facilitated by external agents.

Early Acceptance

PWD's early acceptance by managers and co-workers is important because it impacts integration, the organizational culture and the experience and outcomes of teams that include PWD. Multiple factors influence acceptance of PWD in the organization, among others PWD's attitude toward the organizational culture, acceptance of organizational policies, avoidance of being pitied and support of co-worker perceptions (Bam & Ronnie, 2020). Unexpected outcomes of isolation leading to low job performance and satisfaction are overcome when PWD are included in organizational events and inclusive policies supporting diversity early in their employment as expressed in UD Principle 1.

Working communities as those proposed in this chapter are key to offsetting power and privilege and fostering respect for diversity (Shanahan & Hyman, 2003). To avoid conflict and isolation, internal organizational policies and culture serve as guidelines to be exceeded, not merely to be met. Consistent with Aristotle's theory, Mele (2009) argued that acceptance of the objective existence of a person and lived experiences contribute to personalize the experience of virtue. In contrast, evidence of pity, as opposed to empathy, delays the acceptance of PWD at the integration stage. In contrast with some studies focused on lowering managers' expectations (von Schrader, Malzer, & Bruyère, 2014), our virtue framework proposes that regardless of expectations, PWD should adapt and adopt performance standards guided to integrate smoothly in the organizational culture, as shown in UD Principle 6. The aspirations to meet or exceed the standards of others have potential to result in further injury when not properly managed. In virtuous organizations, managers should be models of proper ambition (Aristotle, 1955).

Developing an Inclusive Organizational Culture

Organizational practices should be consistent with policy intentions to promote and advance the organizational mission. Effective implementation of policies is achieved when PWD are supported to participate proactively in the design of ongoing processes (Gröschl, 2007). Our experience shows that long-term employment satisfaction is highly correlated with how managers and coworkers interpret policies and share values consistent with the Human Centered Organizational Culture principles (Lepeley, 2017, Ochoa et al., 2019).

Managers who embody temperance (Aristotle, 1955) and adopt informal mentoring roles with patience are more effective to provide support and integrate PWD into organizations. Drake, Meckler, and Stephens (2002) similarly recommended that leaders within organizations should intuitively provide help and nurture relationships to the point of support (UD Principle 3) as these initiatives would be welcomed by PWD.

Work environment plays a critical role creating a culture of inclusion that benefits all employees and their wellbeing (Ochoa et al., 2019). Organizations that promote decision-making supported by the working communities can become more attentive to the needs of PWD. We advocate establishing working communities and policy design that enhance virtues, sensitivity, understanding and empathy (Shanahan & Hyman, 2003). High integration of top-to-bottom and bottom-up is a necessary condition to develop increased support for internal organizational policies and external organizational policies sustaining CSR necessary to attract qualified and skilled PWD with potential to enhance workplace diversity and organizational performance.

PWD can become highly integrated in organizations and enhance a hallmark of virtuousness (Arjoon, 2000) when organizations design flexible (UD Principle 2) and equitable (UD Principle 1) policies that ensure PWD create greater value for the business with their work. Business can demonstrate that PWD can add value to the workplace supported by virtuous practices of inclusion, enhanced PWD commitment to their jobs and develop their motivation to succeed which is critically important to promote participation of PWD in the national workforce.

Adding Benefits for Organizations, PWD, and the Broader Society

Organizational Impact and Effects

The relationship between the benefits accrued by the organizations and PWD are linked to a culture of inclusion. Evidence of organizations that transgress fundamental ethical economic principles and overwhelmingly exceed profit-seeking goals with potential to harm the wellbeing on people in the workplace have greater propensity to fail in the 21st century and are inconsistent with the Human Centered Organizational Culture and the human at the center economic framework (Lepeley, 2017, 2019a, b, Ochoa et al., 2019). Solomon (1992) suggested that discussing the economic imperative of organizations is unavoidable, but the need to focus on the individual within the organization and the ethical framework of operation is critical for organizations to attain long-term sustainability (Lepeley, 2017).

In ethical organizations, managers, co-workers and PWD collaborate at work and to improve their communities extending collective benefits beyond exclusive monetary and legalistic enrichment (Bam & Ronnie, 2020). In increasing numbers of thriving working communities, decision-makers are acting with the courage Aristotle identified which is mutually beneficial for workers and the organization (1955). Moral managers (Whetstone, 2003) and human centered leaders (Majluf & Abarca, 2021) play a meaningful role in the promotion of values and assuming responsibility for their ethical actions. Trust and truthfulness are required from all members of the community (Aristotle, 1955), but organizational leaders and managers are clearer examples of intangible benefits that make possible the sustainability of the organization.

In the human centered and ethical framework proposed, managers and workers share responsibility for long-term organizational sustainability aligned with the effects of their actions and decisions in the entire organization. Organizations benefit deploying best practices that integrate PWD in organizational processes of the human centered culture interwoven in an environment of inclusion. As previously emphasized, law compliance does not ensure a climate for inclusion. A voluntary approach of members working in the organization driven by virtues and ethical standards established by managers, co-workers and PWD can meet moral obligations uncodified by laws.

Oliver and Barnes (2006) contend that PWD should be active participants helping organizations to design approaches easy to integrate in legal frameworks. Our framework proposes that organizations need to pursue outcomes connecting PWD expectations with virtuous behavior to improve organizational performance and productivity necessary to attain sustainability with high potential to support development of inclusive societies. Barclay et al. (2012) considered UD to be illustrative of the Aristotelean virtue framework needed to ensure smooth PWD inclusion in organizations to spread and legitimize active PWD involvement across organizations in all sectors and worldwide.

Individual and Societal Outcomes

Increasing participation of PWD in work environments that are accessible and promote their integration (UD Principle 7) leads to inclusive participation that foster human wellbeing and advances the organization mission. PWD who participate in working communities can play active roles as citizens when attention to their impairments and associated pain that some PWD experience is diminished. Solomon (1994), drawing on Aristotle's virtues, promoted the value of citizenship across communities and the labor force to positively impact broader society. Williams and Mavin (2012) proposed similar active citizenship as a means of developing more life opportunities. Through gaining employment, PWD can cope better with their impairments and the financial constraints often imposed on them.

Human centered organizations align with Aristotelian ethical principles to open overdue opportunities for integration of PWD in the workplace. Rai (2015) cautions organizations promoting virtuous principles to pay special attention to excessive workloads with potential to have negative impact on working conditions. These may have detrimental effects on PWD because inefficient management of health issues affects them disproportionally. These effects may extend to the broader community and society at large, considering that PWD can remain financially independent if their health is properly managed in alignment with appropriate working conditions. UD poses that PWD need to decide about options to continue their employment when they confront challenges and are unable to meet work expectations (UD Principle 6).

Furthermore, deployment of the virtue framework implies that an inclusive climate is improved with social networks that help PWD gain access to and retain employment when they seek alternate employment. Ali, Schur, and Blanck (2011) noted a positive impact on society as social networks help to improve the social skills of PWD. The skills they gained at work benefit PWD when they are able to transfer acquired knowledge to their life, which, in turn, results in an overall benefit for society.

Conclusion

All modern organizational models focused on human being and ethical principles and practices reinforce the deployment of organizational cultures that promote integration, diversity and inclusion. Ensuring equal opportunities for all helps organizations and businesses to operate consistently with the Aristotelian virtue framework, supported by UD, applying HCM that in the 21st century is essential to create sustainable inclusive and diverse organizations that are more competitive, innovative and offer more benefits to customers, all workers and their communities.

The UD framework presented in this chapter encourages and facilitates development and deployment of virtuous practices that can effectively integrate PWD preparing them during pre-employment, early employment and assisting organizations to develop the most appropriate PWD culture and active engagement of managers and all workers fostering inclusive human centered workplaces. The approach shared in this chapter shows the positive impact that human centered virtuous organizations entrust to promote diversity and inclusiveness to foster well-being in the workplace as antecedent to project same benefits to communities and society at large.

References

Ali, M., Schur, L., & Blanck, P. (2011). What types of jobs do people with disabilities want? *Journal of Occupational Rehabilitation*, *21*(2), 199–210. http://doi.org/10.1007/s10926-010-9266-0.

Araten-Bergman, T. (2016). Managers' hiring intentions and the actual hiring of qualified workers with disabilities. *The International Journal of Human Resource Management*, *27*(14), 1510–1530. doi: 10.1080/09585192.2015.1128466.

Aristotle (1955). *The Ethics of Aristotle. The Nicomachean Ethics* (J. A. K. Thomson, Trans.). Penguin Classics.

Arjoon, S. (2000). Virtue theory as a dynamic theory of business. *Journal of Business Ethics*, *28*(2), 159–178. Retrieved from http://link.springer.com/article/10.1023/A:1006339112331.

Bam, A., & Ronnie, L. (2018, September). Persons with disabilities and their access to employment in the South African workplace: An exploratory study. *12th International Business Conference*, Mauritius. ISBN 978-0-6399779-0-4

Bam, A., & Ronnie, L. (2020). Inclusion at the workplace: An exploratory study of people with disabilities in South Africa. *International Journal of Disability Management*, *15*(e6), 1–9. 10.1017/idm.2020.5

Barclay, L. A., Markel, K. S., & Yugo, J. E. (2012). Virtue theory and organizations: Considering persons with disabilities. *Journal of Managerial Psychology*, *27*(4), 330–346. http://doi.org/10.1108/02683941211220153.

Buys, N. J., & Rennie, J. (2001). Developing relationships between vocational rehabilitation agencies and employers. *Rehabilitation Counseling Bulletin*, *44*(2), 95–103. http://doi.org/Doi 10.1177/003435520104400206.

Centre for Excellence in Universal Design (2020). *What is Universal Design.* Retrieved from http://universaldesign.ie/What-is-Universal-Design/

Dolmage, J. T. (2017). *Academic Ableism: Disability and Higher Education.* Michigan, USA: University of Michigan Press.

Drake, B. H., Meckler, M., & Stephens, D. (2002). Transitional ethics: Responsibilities of supervisors for supporting employee development. *Journal of Business Ethics*, *38*(1–2), 141–155. http://doi.org/10.1023/A:1015785316253.

Gotsis, G., & Kortezi, Z. (2013). Ethical paradigms as potential foundations of diversity management initiatives in business organizations. *Journal of Organizational Change Management*, *26*(6), 948–976. http://doi.org/10.1108/JOCM-11-2012-0183.

Gröschl, S. (2007). An exploration of HR policies and practices affecting the integration of persons with disabilities in the hotel industry in major Canadian tourism destinations. *International Journal of Hospitality Management*, *26*(3), 666–686. http://doi.org/10.1016/j.ijhm.2006.05.007.

Holmqvist, M. (2009). Complicating the organization: A new prescription for the learning organization? *Management Learning*, *40*(3), 275–287. http://doi.org/10.1177/1350507609104340.

Kalef, L., Barrera, M., & Heymann, J. (2014). Developing inclusive employment: Lessons from Telenor Open Mind. *Work*. http://doi.org/10.3233/WOR-131783

Kulkarni, M., & Kote, J. (2014). Increasing employment of people with disabilities: The role and views of disability training and placement agencies. *Employee Responsibilities and Rights Journal*, *26*(3), 177–193. http://doi.org/10.1007/s10672-013-9216-z.

Lepeley, M. T., Kuschel, K., Beutell, N., Pouw, N. & Eijdenberg, E. (eds.). (2020). *Wellbeing of Women in Entrepreneurship. A Global Perspective.* UK: Routledge.

Lepeley, M. T. (2019a). *EDUCONOMY. Unleashing Wellbeing and Human Centered Sustainable Development.* Information Age Publishing.

Lepeley, M. T. (2019b). *EDUQUALITY. Human Centered Quality Management in Education. A Model for Deployment, Assessment and Sustainability.* Information Age Publishing.

Lepeley, M. T. (2017). *Human Centered Management: The 5 Pillars of Organizational Quality and Global Sustainability.* UK: Routledge.

Mace, R. (1997). *What is Universal Design.* The Center for Universal Design at North Carolina State University.

MacIntyre, A. (2007). *After Virtue: A Study in Moral Theory* (3rd ed.). Notre Dame, Indiana: University of Notre Dame Press. Retrieved from http://www3.undpress.nd.edu/excerpts/P01162-ex.pdf.

Majluf, N., & Abarca, N. (2021). *The Human Centered Leader: Sensible, Insightful, and Prudent.* Part of Human Centered Management Trilogy. Human Centered Management Book Series. US: Routledge .

Markel, K. S., & Barclay, L. A. (2009). Addressing the underemployment of persons with disabilities: Recommendations for expanding organizational social responsibility. *Employee Responsibilities and Rights Journal*, *21*(4), 305–318. http://doi.org/10.1007/s10672-009-9125-3.

McFarlin, D. B., Song, J., & Sonntag, M. (1991). Integrating the disabled into the work force: A survey of Fortune 500 attitudes and practices. *Employee Responsibilities and Rights Journal*, *4*(2), 107–123.

Mele, D. (2009). Integrating personalism into virtue-based business ethics: The personalist and the common good principles. *Journal of Business Ethics*, *88*, 227–244. http://doi.org/10.1007/s10551-009-0108-y

Moore, G. (2005). Humanizing business: A modern virtue ethics approach. *Business Ethics Quarterly*, *15*(2), 237–255.

Ochoa, P., Lepeley, M. T. & Essens, P. (Eds). (2019). *Wellbeing for Sustainability in the Global Workforce*. UK: Routledge.

Oliver, M., & Barnes, C. (2006). *Disability politics and the disability movement in Britain: Where did it all go wrong?* Retrieved from http://citeseerx.ist.psu.edu/viewdoc/download?doi=10.1.1.464.6659&rep=rep1&type=pdf

Pope, D., & Bambra, C. (2005). Has the disability discrimination act closed the employment gap? *Disability and Rehabilitation*, *27*(20), 1261–1266. doi: 10.1080/09638280500075626.

Rai, G. S. (2015). Organizational justice and quality of working life: A road that leads to a virtuous organization. *Journal of Social Service Research*, *41*(2), 269–294. http://doi.org/10.1080/01488376.2014.987942.

Robert, P. M., & Harlan, S. L. (2006). Mechanisms of disability discrimination in large bureaucratic organizations: Ascriptive inequalities in the workplace. *The Sociological Quarterly*, *47*(4), 599–630. doi: 10.1111/j.1533-8525.2006.00060.x.

Schur, L., Kruse, D., & Blasi, J. (2009). Is disability disabling in all workplaces? Workplace disparities and corporate culture. *Industrial Relations*, *48*(3), 381–410.

Shanahan, K. J., & Hyman, M. R. (2003). The development of a virtue ethics scale. *Journal of Business Ethics*, *42*(2), 197–208. http://doi.org/10.1023/A:1021914218659.

Solomon, R. (1992). Corporate roles, personal virtues: An Aristotelean approach to business ethics. *Business Ethics Quarterly*, *2*(3), 317–339.

Solomon, R. (1994). The corporation as community: A reply to Ed Hartman. *Business Ethics Quarterly*, *4*(3), 271. http://doi.org/10.2307/3857447.

Solomon, R. C. (1999). *A Better Way to Think about Business*. Oxford, UK: Oxford University Press.

Thomas, A. (2003). Employment equity practices at selected companies in South Africa. *South African Journal of Labour Relations*. Retrieved from http://reference.sabinet.co.za/sa_epublication_article/labour_v27_n3_4_a2

von Schrader, S., Malzer, V., & Bruyère, S. M. (2014). Perspectives on disability disclosure: The importance of employer practices and workplace climate. *Employee Responsibilities and Rights Journal*, *26*(4), 237–255. https://doi.org/10.1007/s10672-013-9227-9.

Whetstone, J. T. (2003). The language of managerial excellence: Virtues as understood and applied. *Journal of Business Ethics*, *33*(2001), 343–357.

Williams, J., & Mavin, S. (2012). Disability as constructed difference: A literature review and research agenda for management and organization studies. *International Journal of Management Reviews*, *14*(2), 159–179. http://doi.org/10.1111/j.1468-2370.2012.00329.x.

Part II

Human Centered Organizational Culture in Business

7 Assessment of the Theoretical Evolution of Organizational Culture

Pending Need for Human Focus

Oswaldo Morales, Gareth Rees, Sergio Morales

Introduction

This chapter presents a theoretical overview of seven decades in the evolution of the tradition of the Organizational Culture (OC) concept from the perspective of the following notable authors, Pettigrew, Ott, Schein, Denison and Alvesson. This chapter has a dual purpose. To review the importance of OC in organizational development and management, and also to compare their theories how they diverge from the traditional human resource (HR)/human resource management models of the industrial past and to what extent they convergence and align with the new human centered paradigm embedded in Human Centered Management (HCM) model (Lepeley, 2017).

In the 21st century, organizations are affected by disruptions from a global volatility, uncertainty, complexity and ambiguity (VUCA) environment. Constant change presses organizations to assess old structures and evaluate the costs of perpetuating the status quo against the benefits to advance a human focus as a necessary condition for attaining high productivity, competitiveness and long-term sustainability. It is in this sense that Lepeley's HCM reveals as an OC approach for the future to reclaim the importance of people at the center of OCs worldwide.

Assessment and Evolution of the OC Concept

Andrew Pettigrew and the Origin of OC

Four decades ago, Pettigrew defined culture as a system of public and collective accepted meanings operating for a given group at a given time and introduced through concepts such as symbols, language, ideology, belief, ritual and myth to illustrate aspects of *cultural and expressive components of organizational life* (1979). Although widely used in anthropology, these concepts were not integrated into the mainstream of organizational theory. According to Pettigrew, the value of cultural components was related to the creation of new cultures and how managers provide order, purpose and commitment to organizations. Likewise, OC conceived as *patterns of meanings and consciousness* is generated by the feelings and actions of founders, therefore *the essential problem of entrepreneurship is the translation of individual drive into collective purpose and commitment* (Pettigrew, 1979).

For Ehrhart, Schneider, and Macey (2014), Pettigrew's essay demonstrated the application of anthropological methods and concepts to the study of organizations at a time when business studies showed an unprecedented focus on human behavior. In this context, management consultants discovered the importance of studying organizations including the experiences of all their members (Ehrhart et al., 2014). Pettigrew's essay was important because he defined culture as a collection of concepts, analyzed its evolution over time and developed the functional role in terms of integration, management and commitment, highlighting the role of founder's in the firm imprint (Ehrhart et al., 2014). As such, Pettigrew's work demarcated *the beginning of contemporary scholarly interest in the topic* (Ehrhart et al., 2014).

For Ehrhart et al., Pettigrew *formally introduced the anthropological study of cultures to the organizational research literature, in stark contrast to the individually focused psychological research on organizational climate* (2014). Similarly, for Schneider and Barbera (2014), Pettigrew's essay *stimulated attention to a culture perspective on organizational life* considering *organizations as human entities and not just as financial institutions or operational settings for productivity alone* (Schneider & Barbera, 2014).

The 1980s and the Popularization of OC

In the 1980s, five books enhanced the importance of culture in business: *Theory Z* (Ouchi, 1981), *The Art of Japanese Management* (Pascale & Athos, 1981), *In Search of Excellence* (Peters & Waterman, 1982), *Corporate Cultures* (Deal & Kennedy, 1982) and *The Change Masters* (Kanter, 1983). According to Denison (1990), these books provided a different image of management demonstrating that *the difference between successful and unsuccessful organizations rests in the values and principles that underlie the internal organization*. Due to its impact, OC was considered *one of the most powerful and stable forces operating in organizations* (Schein, 1996, p. 231).

For Ehrhart et al. (2014), these contributions emphasized *symbolic aspects of organizational life and the importance of creating shared values at all levels of the organization*. They also showed that when leaders manage values correctly, culture becomes *a source of competitive advantage, differentiating it from its competitors and resulting in improved organizational effectiveness and productivity* (Ehrhart et al., 2014).

J. Steven Ott and the OC Perspective

In *The Organizational Culture Perspective*, Ott (1989) argued that studying OC implies using *a different set of «lenses» to «see» an organization*, a notion that refers to a *way of looking and thinking about behavior in organizations [and] a perspective for understanding what is occurring*. For Ott, this *organizational culture perspective* constitutes a *counterculture* because its *assumptions, theories, and approaches are different from the dominant structural and systems perspectives*" (1989). However, this approach *does not believe that quantitative, experimental-type, logical-positivist, scientific research is useful to study organizations* as it embodies *the newest and perhaps the most controversial of the organization theory perspectives* (Ott, 1989).

According to such perspective, the behavior of the members of an organization are not controlled by rules or forms of authority but cultural norms, values, beliefs and assumptions. Therefore, *in order to understand or predict how an organization will behave under different circumstances, one must know what* its *patterns of basic assumptions are* – its *organizational culture* (Ott, 1989). In this respect, the OC perspective not only uses qualitative techniques (such as ethnography or participant observation), but also considers that, in their attempts to understand and predict organizational behavior, the structuralist and systemic theories use *wrong lenses* to analyze the *wrong organizational elements* and its tools are as ineffective as *a hammer is for fixing a leaking pipe*; which is why *they are wasting their time* (Ott, 1989).

At the time, Ott indicated there were five points of consensus on cultures of organizations, namely: (i) they exist, (ii) they are *relatively unique*, (iii) they are *socially constructed*, (iv) they provide a *way of understanding* and are *making sense* and (v) they constitute a *powerful lever* for organizational behavior (1989).

Although, Ott argued that the OC *is not something easily broken down into elements and placed in single boxes* and since their essential functions do not differ, he proposed a *functional definition* that conceived OC as *a social force that controls patterns of organizational behavior by shaping members' cognitions and perceptions of meanings and realities, providing affective energy for mobilization, and identifying who belongs and who does not* (Ott, 1989).

Edgar Schein and His Influence on the OC Literature

In *Organizational Culture and Leadership*, Schein developed what would become *the most commonly cited definition* (Ehrhart et al., 2014) of culture as a *pattern of shared basic assumptions the group learns to solve problems of external adaptation and internal integration* (1992).

Distancing himself from previous definitions, Schein argued that his definition of culture does not refer to overt behavior or material artifacts but emphasizes *the critical assumptions to deal with how to perceive, think about, and feel about things* (1992).

Schein's conceptualization presents two basic features. First, the fundamental role of the firm's founder. According to Schein, the sources of beliefs and values *by far most important for cultural beginnings, is the impact of founders.* Likewise starting an organization, the founders *usually have major impact on how the group initially defines and solves external adaptation and internal integration challenges.* So how big is the impact? To transmit assumptions and values, the founder engages in an *embedding* process of cultural elements. Therefore, during the firm's initial stages, *most of the culture is likely to be a reflection of the founder's personality* (Schein, 1992).

Second, OC is built on three levels: artifacts, espoused values and basic underlying assumptions (Schein, 1992). First, artifacts refer to observed phenomena, basically overt behavior. For Schein, *the most important point about this level of the culture is that it is easy to observe but difficult to decipher.* Second, the shared values the group shares guide their behavior and result from the influence of the founder or leader. For Schein, *leadership is the source of beliefs and values.*

Third, basic underlying assumptions refer to those implicit that constitute the essence of culture. For Schein, *culture is a set of basic assumptions that defines what to pay attention to, what things mean, how to react emotionally to what is going on, and what actions to take in various kinds of situations.* As such, Schein contends that *to understand the culture of a group, attempts must be made to understand shared basic assumptions and the learning process underlying the basic assumptions* (1992).

As an organizational psychology scholar, Schein pointed out that *many of the research methods of industrial/organizational psychology expose weaknesses applied to the analysis of culture* (1990). Schein, therefore, advised that studying culture, researchers need to adopt a more clinical and ethnographic approach for identifying the dimensions and variables that provide empirical measurement for hypothesis testing (Schein, 1990).

For Schein, *culture is not only all around us but within us as well,* therefore, by using cultural lenses implies deciphering of the cultural forces that operate in groups, organizations and occupations (2010). The most peculiar aspect of culture is that *it points to phenomena that are below the surface, that are powerful in their impact but invisible and to a considerable degree unconscious* (Schein, 2010).

In a recent work, Schein and Schein (2017) added to Schein's original definition arguing that culture refers to *accumulated shared learning of a group to solve problems of external adaptation and internal integration.*

As such, culture covers everything that a group has learned while it evolves and consequently *the strength of the culture depends on the length of time, the stability of membership, and the emotional intensity of the actual historical learning experiences they have shared* (Schein & Schein, 2017).

Denison on OC and Effectiveness

In *Corporate Culture and Organizational Effectiveness*, Denison (1990) defined OC as those underlying values, beliefs and principles that serve as a foundation for an organization's management system and the set of management practices and behaviors that exemplify and reinforce the basic principles. For Denison, a cultural theory of organizational effectiveness must recognize that the values, beliefs and meanings that underlie a social group are *the primary source of motivated and coordinated activity*, supporting Schein's idea that the study of OC should rely on the use of ethnographic methods (1990).

Denison offered a variation from Schein's definition but similarly proposed a three-level model of culture composed of values and beliefs underlying actions, behavioral patterns that reflect and reinforce values and a set of conditions created by behavioral patterns. Emphasizing a pragmatic character, Denison's typology *focuses more on concrete actions, conditions, and practices rooted in an organization's value system* and pointing out that *the most positive impact of the cultural perspective is that it represents a return to inductive thinking about the behavioral characteristics of organizations* (1990).

Mats Alvesson and the Meaning Notion of OC

In *Understanding Organizational Culture (2002)*, Alvesson argued that the main achievement of OC is to verify that the cultural dimension is central in all aspects of the organizational life and it is highly significant for the functioning of organizations. Considering culture as *central* in understanding of behavior, social events, institutions and processes, then the best way to study it is through the notion of meaning because for Alvesson *meaning makes an object relevant and meaningful* (2002).

Alvesson argued that to guide thought, feelings and actions in a cultural context, the most important thing is shared meanings. Thus, a *cultural understanding* of organizations does not emphasize *individual idiosyncrasies* collective meanings that include *the experiences of people* and connect *the organization as with everyday experiences and individual action* (2002). In other words, culture becomes *significant as a bond holding the organization together*. Alvesson warns that *trying to do so may implicate a simplistic view of culture underestimating* its *theoretical potential and value* (2002). Likewise, conceiving culture pragmatically constitutes an *offensive formulation* suggesting that OC can be used as *a tool or guiding concept for achieving effectiveness*, while seeing it as *an obstacle to economic rationality and effectiveness* is a *defensive version* of the culture-performance relationship (Alvesson, 2002).

From a critical perspective, Alvesson stated that *the purpose of cultural studies is liberating human potential or illuminating the obstacles of emancipation* (2002). Thus, the objective of cultural analysis is *to encourage critical reflection on beliefs, values, and understandings of social conditions* (Alvesson, 2002). Alvesson attributes OC a critical role that affirms an *understanding of cultural management*, not as a technocratic project but where an interpretive company *may reduce the gap between a technical, a practical-hermeneutic and an emancipatory approach to organizational culture* and because it provides *deep thinking* on organizational life, and that *cultural interpretation as* oneof *the best ways of understanding a broad spectrum of aspects of management and organizations* (2002).

From these summaries, we see that the five authors' view of an organization's culture is established in the values of its founders and develops through the shared and learned experiences of its member overtime. From their perspectives, OC is not simply a set of instructions drafted for intent or to direct. Rather, it is implicit and explicit how culture exerts its influence over the organization as a whole and its members individually. It has a powerful effect that cannot be overcome through directives from above or the enforcement of rules from the outside with an enduring character that it is difficult to extinguish. This is the reason why OC has had some bearing on other branches of management theory and practice.

OC and Its Contribution to Organizational Theory

The concept of culture has contributed to organizational theory directing attention to *new phenomena in the organization expanding the field of study* (Schultz, 1994). Concepts such as myth, metaphor, ritual, stories, ceremonies or ethos were incorporated providing new interpretations of already known phenomena. For example, the strategic plan is not only a forum for decision-making but also a *signal* of the importance of the future. And the informal organization is not only a *routinized behavioral pattern* but also a *cultural network* where *priests, spies, storytellers and 'support clubs'* transmit fundamental values (Schultz, 1994). Schein also observes that *organization studies will not mature as a field until more time is spent observing and absorbing other cultures* (1996).

OC has had a wide imprint, impacting many areas of organizational theory, including leadership (Schein & Schein, 2017), structure (Janićijević, 2013), knowledge management (Chang & Lin, 2015), symbolism (Alvesson & Berg, 1992), change (Alvesson & Sveningsson, 2016), effectiveness

(Hartnell, Ou, & Kinicki, 2011), performance (Boyce, Nieminen, Gillespie, Ryan, & Denison, 2015), ethical behavior (Kuye, Uche, & Akaighe, 2013), national culture (Hofstede, Hofstede, & Minkov, 2010), information systems (Jackson, 2011), continuous improvement (Timmerman, 2019) and, even, corruption (Campbell & Göritz, 2014).

OC and Business Management

According to Ehrhart et al., there is no one best way to study OC and with so many factors influencing and influenced by culture, the analysis is complex (2014). For Alvesson *all management takes place within a culture* (2002). OC impacts across business activities, impacting all people, personnel management policies (Aycan, Kanungo, & Sinha, 1999), recruitment practices (Gardner, Reithel, Cogliser, Walumbwa, & Foley, 2012), personnel selection (Burk & Birk, 2001), employee retention and remunerations (Sheridan, 1992), communication (Keyton, 2005), job satisfaction assessment (Lund, 2003), conflict management (Di Pietro & Di Virgilio, 2013), job burnout (Kheirandish, Farahani, & Nikkhoo, 2016), customer satisfaction (Gillespie, Denison, Haaland, Smerek, & Neale, 2008), commitment and work engagement (Miroshnik, 2013), competitiveness (Gómez-Miranda, Pérez-López, Argente-Linares, & Rodríguez-Ariza, 2015), brand identity (Rashid & Ghose, 2015), innovation (Naranjo-Valencia, Jiménez-Jiménez, & Sanz-Valle, 2011) and mergers and acquisitions (Morales, 2015). OC is relevant to organizations in all industries and sectors such as health (Mannion & Davies, 2018), basic education (Deal & Peterson, 2016) and higher education (Lacatus, 2013), construction (Coffey, 2010) to name a few.

Pending Need: People-Centered OC

Given the changes in societies and disruptions of all kinds in the global VUCA environment, it is necessary to think if OC will remain as relevant in the future. For Maitland and Thomson, the outcome will depend on the capacity of people in organizations to design and transform an OC aligned with technologies that support and promote work engagement and success. General conditions show that the work of the future will require significant transformation of the traditional OC (2014). Considering that leaders are mainly responsible for changes in culture, then identifying the needed transformation will be increasingly a key responsibility for leaders, executives and senior management (Maitland & Thomson, 2014). In *The Flow of Organizational Culture (2020)*, MacQueen states that there are few things more abstract and difficult to understand than OC. This is a warning challenge for leaders today and in the future.

In the present environment, increasing numbers of scholars are emphasizing the human dimension of OC. This is reflected in a changing terminology replacing the traditional term HRs with personnel (Aycan *et al.* 1999; Burk & Birk, 2001). This change is largely due to an increasing interest for people's wellbeing in studies covering a wide range of dimensions that goes beyond business and organizations in general but also at national and international levels. In the last decades, the human dimension has been propelled by initiatives of international development organizations, including the United Nations and the World Bank, and increasing numbers of studies focusing on happiness and wellbeing (Lepeley et al., 2020, Ochoa, Lepeley, & Essens, 2019, Lepeley, 2017a, Helliwel & Putnam, 2004). Their interests project a new vision of organizations calling attention to the wellbeing of people in the organizational context that until recently was unheard of.

Alvesson (2002) stated that any form of management is increasingly linked to an OC in transition from a hierarchical and bureaucratic organization resource to a flatter organization with a human centered structure.

Ott conveyed that the behavior of the members of an organization is not controlled by rules, norms or forms of authority but by cultural norms, values, beliefs and the assumptions of people (1989). Ott's ideas about OC aimed to promote responsible behavior to enhance wellbeing in the workplace converge with the foundations of Lepeley's HCM model and the human centered paradigm shift she has pioneered (2017).

Schein and Schein (2017) defined culture as the accumulated shared learning of a group solving problems of external adaptation and internal integration. Their binary organizational vision is consistent with HCM principles synchronizing internal organizational imperatives embedded in the inward-looking structure with an outward-looking vision looking at external demands shaped by consumers and influenced by market forces in the community where the organization is inserted. These are the drives molding Social Corporate Responsibility (Lepeley, 2017). These human centered principles align optimal synchrony of the needs and demands of customers with the needs of the people who work in the organization and produce products and services (Lepeley, 2017).

The concepts developed by Pettigrew, Ott, Schein, Denison and Alvesson provided the seeds to make the transition from traditional resource perspectives toward the human centered perspective embedded in the HCM paradigm (Lepeley, 2017).

References

Alvesson, M. (2002). *Understanding Organizational Culture*. London: SAGE.

Alvesson, M., & Berg, P. (1992). *Corporate Culture and Organizational Symbolism*. Berlin: De Gruyter.

Alvesson, M., & Sveningsson, S. (2016). *Changing Organizational Culture: Cultural Change Work in Progress*. New York: Routledge.

Aycan, Z., Kanungo, R., & Sinha, J. (1999). Organizational culture and human resource practices: The model of culture fit. *Journal of Cross-Cultural Psychology*, *30*(4), 501–526.

Bardy, R. (2016). Conjoining competition and morality. Six teaching blocks for building human centered organizations. In M. T. Lepeley, E. von Kimakowitz, & R. Bardy, *Human Centered Management in Executive Education: Global Imperatives, Innovation, and New Directions* (pp. 273–290). Basingstoke: Palgrave Macmillan.

Boyce, A., Nieminen, L., Gillespie, M., Ryan, A., & Denison, D. (2015). Which comes first, organizational culture or performance? A longitudinal study of causal priority with automobile dealerships. *Journal of Organizational Behavior*, *36*(3), 339–359.

Burk, J., & Birk, T. (2001). The art and science of personnel selection: Assessing "goodness of fit" with organizational culture. *Performance Improvement*, *40*(1), 32–37.

Campbell, J., & Göritz, A. (2014). Culture corrupts! A qualitative study of organizational culture in corrupt organizations. *Journal of Business Ethics*, *120*(3), 291–311.

Chang, C., & Lin, T. (2015). The role of organizational culture in the knowledge management process. *Journal of Knowledge Management*, *19*(3), 433–455.

Coffey, V. (2010). *Understanding Organisational Culture in the Construction Industry*. New York: Taylor & Francis.

Deal, T., & Kennedy, A. (1982). *Corporate Cultures: The Rites and Rituals of Corporate Life*. Boston: Addison-Wesley.

Deal, T., & Peterson, K. (2016). *Shaping School Culture*. San Francisco: Jossey-Bass.

Denison, D. (1990). *Corporate Culture and Organizational Effectiveness*. New York: Wiley.

Di Pietro, L., & Di Virgilio, F. (2013). The role of organizational culture on informal conflict management. *International Journal of Public Administration*, *36*(13), 910–921.

Edmonds, S. C. (2014). *The Culture Engine. A Framework for Driving Results, Inspiring Your Employees, and Transforming Your Workplace*. Hoboken: John Wiley & Sons, Inc.

Ehrhart, M., Schneider, B., & Macey, W. (2014). *Organizational Climate and Culture*. New York: Routledge.

Friedman, R. (2014). *The Best Place to Work: The Art and Science of Creating an Extraordinary Workplace*. New York: Penguin Group.

Gardner, W., Reithel, B., Cogliser, C., Walumbwa, F., & Foley, R. (2012). Matching personality and organizational culture: Effects of recruitment strategy and the Five-Factor model of subjective person–organization fit. *Management Communication Quarterly*, *26*(4), 585–622.

Gillespie, M., Denison, D., Haaland, S., Smerek, R., & Neale, W. (2008). Linking organizational culture and customer satisfaction: Results from two companies in different industries. *European Journal of Work and Organizational Psychology*, *17*(1), 112–132.

Gómez-Miranda, M., Pérez-López, M., Argente-Linares, E., & Rodríguez-Ariza, L. (2015). The impact of organizational culture on competitiveness, effectiveness and efficiency in Spanish-Moroccan international joint ventures. *Personnel Review*, *44*(3), 364–387.

Hartnell, C., Ou, A., & Kinicki, A. (2011). Organizational culture and organizational effectiveness: A meta-analytic investigation of the competing values framework's theoretical suppositions. *Journal of Applied Psychology*, *96*(4), 677–694.

Helliwell, J. F., & Putnam, R. D. (2004). The social context of well–being. *Philosophical Transactions of the Royal Society of London. Series B: Biological Sciences*, *359*(1449), 1435–1446.

Hofstede, G., Hofstede, G. J., & Minkov, M. (2010). Cultures and organizations: Software of the mind, *Intercultural cooperation and its importance for survival* (3rd ed.). New York: McGraw-Hill.

Jackson, S. (2011). Organizational culture and information systems adoption: A three-perspective approach. *Information and Organization*, *21*(2), 57–83.

Janićijević, N. (2013). The mutual impact of organizational culture and structure. *Economic Annals*, *58*(198), 35–60.

Kanter, R. (1983). *The Change Masters: Innovation for Productivity in the American Corporation*. New York: Simon & Schuster.

Keyton, J. (2005). *Communication & Organizational Culture: A Key to Understanding Work Experiences*. Thousand Oaks: SAGE.

Kheirandish, M., Farahani, A., & Nikkhoo, B. (2016). The impact of organizational culture on employees' job burnout. *International Academic Journal of Organizational Behavior and Human Resource Management*, *3*(10), 1–15.

Kuye, O., Uche, C., & Akaighe, G. (2013). Organizational culture and ethical behavior: A strategic standpoint. *Journal of Humanities, Social Sciences and Creative Arts*, *8*(1), 1–12.

Lacatus, M. (2013). Organizational culture in contemporary university. *Procedia, Social and Behavioral Sciences*, *76*, 421–425.

Lepeley, M. T., Kuschel, K., Beutell, N., Pouw, N., & Eijdenberg, E. (Eds.). (2020). *Wellbeing of Women in Entrepreneurship. A Global Perspective*. Abingdon, UK: Routledge.

Lepeley, M. T. (2017a). *Human Centered Management. The 5 Pillars of Organization Quality and Global Sustainability*. New York: Routledge.

Lepeley, M. T. (2017b). Bhutan's Gross National Happiness. An approach to human centred sustainable development. *South Asian Journal of Human Resource Management*, *4*(2), 174–184.

Lepeley, M. T., von Kimakowitz, E. & Bardy, R. (Eds). (2016). *Human Centered Management in Executive Education: Global Imperatives, Innovation, and New Directions*. Basingstoke: Palgrave Macmillan.

Lund, D. (2003). Organizational culture and job satisfaction. *Journal of Business & Industrial Marketing*, *18*(3), 219–236.

MacQueen, J. (2020). *The Flow of Organizational Culture: New Thinking and Theory for Better Understanding and Process*. Cham: Palgrave Macmillan.

Maitland, A., & Thomson, P. (2014). *Future Work: Changing Organizational Culture for the New World of Work*. Basingstoke: Palgrave Macmillan.

Mannion, R., & Davies, H. (2018). Understanding organisational culture for healthcare quality improvement. *British Medical Journal*, *363*, k4907.

Miroshnik, V. (2013). *Organizational Culture and Commitment*. New York: Palgrave Macmillan.

Morales, O. (2015). La importancia de la cultura organizacional en los procesos de fusiones y adquisiciones. *Tiempo de Opinión*, *5*(8), 44–57.

Naranjo-Valencia, J., Jiménez-Jiménez, D., & Sanz-Valle, R. (2011). Innovation or imitation? The role of organizational culture. *Management Decision*, *49*(1), 55–72.

Ochoa, P., Lepeley, M. T., & Essens, P. (Eds.). (2019). *Wellbeing for Sustainability in the Global Workforce*. Abingdon: Routledge. UK.

Ott, J. S. (1989). *The Organizational Culture Perspective*. Chicago: The Dorsey Press.

Ouchi, W. (1981). *Theory Z: How American Business Can Meet the Japanese Challenge*. New York: Avon Books.

Pascale, R., & Athos, A. (1981). *The Art of Japanese Management: Applications for American Executives*. New York: Simon & Schuster.

Peters, T., & Waterman, R. (1982). *In Search of Excellence: Lessons from America's Best-Run Companies*. New York: Harper Collins.

Pettigrew, A. (1979). On studying organizational cultures. *Administrative Science Quarterly*, *24*(4), 570–581.

Rashid, S., & Ghose, K. (2015). Organisational culture and the creation of brand identity: Retail food branding in new markets. *Marketing Intelligence & Planning*, *33*(1), 2–19.

Schein, E. (1990). Organizational culture. *American Psychologist*, *45*(2), 109–119.

Schein, E. (1992). *Organizational Culture and Leadership*. San Francisco: Jossey-Bass.

Schein, E. (1996). Culture: The missing concept in organization studies. *Administrative Science Quarterly*, *41*(2), 229–240.

Schein, E. (2000). Sense and nonsense about culture and climate. In N. Ashkanasy, C. Wilderon & M. Peterson (Eds.). *Handbook of Organizational Culture & Climate* (pp. xxiii–xxx). Thousand Oaks: SAGE.

Schein, E. (2010). *Organizational Culture and Leadership*. San Francisco: Jossey-Bass.

Schein, E., & Schein, P. (2017). *Organizational Culture and Leadership*. Hoboken: Wiley.

Schneider, B. & Barbera, K. (Eds.). (2014). *The Oxford Handbook of Organizational Climate and Culture*. Oxford: Oxford University Press.

Schultz, M. (1994). *On Studying Organizational Cultures*. Berlin: De Gruyter.

Sheridan, J. (1992). Organizational culture and employee retention. *Academy of Management Journal*, *35*(5), 1036–1056.

Stallard, M. L., Pankau, J., & Stallard, K. P. (2015). *Connection Culture: The Competitive Advantage of Shared Identity, Empathy, and Understanding at Work*. Alexandria, VA: American Society for Training & Development.

Timmerman, B. (2019). *Starting Lean from Scratch: A Senior Leader's Guide to Beginning and Steering an Organizational Culture Change for Continuous Improvement*. New York: Routledge.

8 A Human Centered Organizational Culture

Focused on Wellbeing, Fairness and the Common Good

Nicolas Majluf

COVID-19 and the Global Volatile, Uncertain, Complex and Ambiguous (VUCA) Environment

At the time of this writing, people worldwide have been living one of the most profound disruptions in recent human history. I find myself anchored at home because of the COVID-19 pandemic that is sweeping the world from the beginning of 2020. The news focus on the advance of coronavirus in countries around the world and the precautions people must take to be safe and avoid spreading the virus, including seclusion, social distancing and other hygiene concerns.

This situation has lasted months, and it is far from over (August 2020). Despite the continuous efforts of national authorities and healthcare professionals in the *front line* in Chile, where I live, the pandemic is running its course, with its burden of contagion, critical illnesses and many deaths. This process will go on until a vaccine is discovered to spread immunization and stop contagiousness. Experts and nations are waiting for a *flattening curve* of the disease.

The alteration of life is enormous. Income earning has become uncertain for a large portion of the population. Many have lost their jobs while many others have had their salaries decreased. Businesses are closing, and the few that remain open cannot operate regularly. To get food or medicines is increasingly difficult. Forecasts anticipate a severe global recession unseen since the Great Depression. Substantial losses of people's wellbeing, welfare and income are expected in countries worldwide.

The pandemic is contributing to call increased attention and scrutiny of institutions at the national and international levels. The world's governing institutions' growing instability adds volatility and uncertainty to this global VUCA environment. In this context, ethical dilemmas are demanding. Lifting quarantine restrictions to start the economies is an excruciating quandary. Governments' decision is between losing lives today or avoiding poverty and hunger in the future, pressed by the precarious existence under long confinement.

The Pandemic is Not the Only Crisis

In Chile, the pandemic adds to other complex situations demanding the transformation of the sociopolitical and economic system. But Chile's problems are not unique. Inequality, the discredit of leaders, mistrust of business and political confrontations are present in nations worldwide.

The financial crisis of 2008 put the stability of global institutions at risk. The relevance of that crisis called into question the effectiveness of the current system. Bower, Leonard, and Paine (2011) stated in stark terms indicating that although the economic system has been extraordinarily successful, it needs review and improvement to face current disruptions. If this situation remains as it is, they predict *a bumpy ride or a collapse of the system*. They call business firms to act to remedy this hazardous situation.

There is growing evidence that the single-minded focus on profits hinders business firms' opportunities to foster the common good and long-term wellbeing of people and society. Products and services, such as free access to information, security, an environment free of pollution, food, housing, education, health, work and mobilization, should be available to everyone. Many are the issues that need deep reflection to ensure that the focus of organizational culture is on people's wellbeing.

1 Economic growth must be synchronized with human wellbeing to be sustainable (Lepeley, 2017b). It is not appropriate to assume that economic growth by itself can solve all problems. Increasing depletion of natural resources, climate change and environmental degradation are a consequence of this reasoning. Progress, understood in this way, has no future: it is self-defeating. It is an unsustainable formula inconsistent with Human Centered Management principles and practices. Human wellbeing and economic growth must be aligned. Thinking of people first is a requirement for countries to attain sustainability (Lepeley, 2017a).
2 The globalization of markets has benefited millions of people who have emerged from poverty, but it has produced a growing wealth concentration. Inequality is a source of social and health problems. All people must have possibilities for self-improvement and access to a good life. Today, a large part of humanity lacks opportunities due to their precarious economic situation.
3 The Knowledge Society rewards highly skilled people and experts in handling technologies. But it penalizes the majority who lack these skills, impairing opportunities for inclusive progress and creating barriers to access good jobs. The advances in automation and artificial intelligence exacerbate this situation because it leverages capital investment, limiting further opportunities for people with low skills. Technology advances have aggravated inequality and

weakened middle-income groups. Confronting these issues is a vital responsibility of governments as much as business firms, entrusted with the responsibility of promoting a culture of inclusiveness and participation.

4 The values promoted in society are essential. Having a *healthy ambition* that limits a behavior solely oriented at getting achievements or honors is good. To exaggerate individualism, greed and selfishness as the basis for faster growth is worrying because it undermines the essence of human coexistence. Taken to the extreme, it promotes unbridled accumulation of wealth and encourages corruption.

5 Freedom to choose is certainly a positive value in society. But considering it as a supreme value may be inappropriate. There are limits to behavior. First, the exercise of freedom is within a framework defined by economic, social, legal, political and cultural conditions. The promotion of a self-centered behavior weakens social cohesion, undermines political legitimacy and neglects the common good. Freedom is not synonymous with unruliness or unlimited consumption.

6 Meritocracy is ingrained in the decision-making process of organizations. It is considered a fair rule that promotes good choices. Sandel (2020) warns that meritocracy's social dynamic may be less benign than usually assumed because the competition does not take place on equal terms, helping preserve existing privileges. He says that even if meritocracy worked perfectly and opportunities for advancement were genuinely equitable, it would corrode solidarity.

7 The other point that Sandel (2020) makes is about compensation. He indicates that the pandemic has shown that job salaries are not necessarily related to contribution to the common good. He says that the essential workers in this crisis, besides doctors and nurses, do not require college degrees and have lower pay, such as delivery workers, supermarket cashiers, nurse assistants and many others.

8 We are living a fast-paced life, with no rest or pause. Highly demanding work responsibilities or self-imposed obligations at all levels are hindering our human condition.

An Opportunity to Rethink Life and Work

People worldwide are in the middle of one of the harshest VUCA *environments* of recent times, with high volatility, uncertainty, complexity and ambiguity. The health crisis is accelerating increases in teleworking, telemedicine and distance education.

When facing extreme and unusual situations, it is time to pay closer attention to the essence of life. The urgent question is whether once the circumstances are normalized, people will return to the *old normal* or dare to explore a profoundly different *new normal.*

Some think this is simply a pause, and things will return to the *old normal.* But, given the significant effects of disruptions, this accommodative belief may impair a unique opportunity to review and rebuild on more solid grounds the advance toward new organizations and societies' common good. Juan Arnau Navarro (2020) suggests that the circumstances are so extreme that it is a time for pause and reflection because COVID-19 is testing modern capitalism and questioning our way of life and values.

Humankind seems to be facing a *decisive moment.* It is the occasion to examine new initiatives fostering people's wellbeing, the sustainability and inclusiveness of societies, and the progress of countries worldwide. At the same time, it is an exceptional moment to reconsider the purpose of everything we, as ordinary people, do and redefining the basis of personal behavior, restating how we relate with one another.

Addressing fundamental issues confronts an additional difficulty. The underlying moral perspective affects answers to questions like Who are we? What kind of society do we want? How do we distinguish between right and wrong? Authers (2020) identifies four relevant perspectives that provide very different vantage points of view: John Rawls' Theory of Justice, the Utilitarianism of John Stuart Mill and Jeremy Bentham, the Liberal thinking of John Locke and Ayn Rand and the Communitarianism put forward by the Greek philosophers and by thinkers such as Amitai Etzioni and Michael Sandel.

Business Firms Play a Critical Role in the Economy and Society, But They Need to Advance More Decisively to a Human Centered Culture

Deep political, economic, social, cultural, demographic and technological changes of the last decades have improved people's wellbeing, providing valuable goods and services contributing to a better life. But it has not avoided many people's frustrations and the outrage against business firms of consumers, environmental groups and other social organizations due to unfulfilled expectations and alleged abuses that harm people and benefit a privileged few.

Moreover, public attention and scrutiny of business practices have increased globally to unprecedented levels. The media have abandoned its traditional objective stance, adopting more militant positions. Social networking has brought instantaneous communication and, at the same time, distortions of truth via *fake news*. The *influencers* people who have a disproportionate impact in public opinion by their social networks actions may become very nefarious if they use their power as opinion leaders to preach hate, as they often do.

Although many business firms today are questioned, and their prestige is harmed, countries need them to resolve social needs. Companies *are vital protagonists and actors in the society of the 21st century*...Sustainable *enterprises will not change capitalism but can make it better* (Jauregui, 2020). But two conditions must be met. The first is that companies must be profitable if they are to grow and endure; the second is how profits are generated matters. Porter and Kramer (2011) state that profits that include a social benefit represent a higher form of capitalism and call for businesses to *reconnect economic success with social progress.* Business firms must realize that their subsistence is possible only when they satisfy the demands of all stakeholders. Otherwise, it is hard to give the attention it deserves to the common good and people's wellbeing, thwarting long-term sustainability.

Hence, the challenge is how to build companies that excel at aligning legitimate profits and contributes to enhancing the common good. The answer offered in this chapter is *building a* Human Centered Organizational Culture, along the lines of Lepeley (2017a).

Building the Human Centered Organizational Culture

Confronting a deep crisis provides a golden opportunity to assess new prospects and reinterpret the meaning of development. As Adela Cortina (2020) suggests: *human beings must now consider the future and decide what they want: whether a united society in which all work together to make people better off or one marked by separation and conflict* (Cortina, 2020)

A human centered development integrates economic growth with the wellbeing of people. Interpreting progress exclusively in terms of Gross National Product (GNP) is an incomplete view. Not everything can be summed up in economic variables, although growth, productivity and financial stability certainly matter. But there are other dimensions of development related to human wellbeing that concern the personal, social, moral, spiritual and cultural domains.

Many organizations are producing new measures of development to complement the shortcomings of GNP. The World Bank has defined human development as a core strategy to improve people's lives and support sustainable development.[1] The United Nations defines the Human Development Index (HDI) [2] as a summary evaluation of average achievement in key dimensions of human development, including life expectancy, education and income earning potential to attain a decent standard of living. It also produces the World Happiness Report, written by a group of independent experts from the Gallup World Poll data.[3]

The emphasis on all efforts to complement the GNP measure of development is on integrating new human development indices that provide a more comprehensive view of social progress. A representative list includes poverty prevalence, degree of inequality, social cohesion, quality of education, economic mobility, gender disparity, migrations, human and work security, citizen participation, cultural identity, preservation and care of the environment and water sanitation. The ideal is to use a wide variety of these dimensions, but proposed indices, such as HDI and others, are restricted to partial assessments of what human and social development entails.

The Human Centered Business Firm

For business firms, the challenge is to drive the organization toward people's needs inside and outside it. Although knowledge society's rapid advance is a clear indication of progress, business firms need to go beyond technology to establish their full contribution to society. They need to address the satisfaction of people's most basic needs, such as food, housing, healthcare and safety. And they must also care about essential aspects of wellbeing, such as social relations, intellectual growth, work safety and spiritual needs.

At the core of a successful business firm, there is a community of people with a common organizational culture, shared stories and a single spirit that molds the self. Sharing culture does not mean uniformity. Flourishing organizations value diversity, open minds and provide ample room for experimentation and exploration. This characteristic of a culture is rather *unity in diversity*.

Community life provides a basic framework for human interactions, where trust, collaboration and solidarity are central values. The pandemic has highlighted the importance of human relations when attending to the needs of ailing people. Dr. Ouyang (2020) showed distress when stating that all her medical knowledge was of no use to attend to the needs of patients and their families. The only important thing was *just to be a person* first. All technical and economic resources were insufficient to deal with their grief.

Putting the person first is of the essence in a Human Centered Organizational Culture. Business firms are not merely machines of growth and profitability. They are critical contributors to a better future for all.

Having exclusively short-term profit metrics is a shortsighted harming orientation. Sustainability requires a long-term vision of the organization's impact on society. The way of doing business for the last 30 years is not attuned to societal expectations today. Firms must look for new ways of doing business, in which ethics and the concern for people are central. And this is an urgent task.

This call has been clearly behind the influential 2019 Redefinition *of the* Purpose *of a* Corporation of the Business Roundtable and the 2020 *Davos Manifesto* of the World Economic Forum.[4] Their proposals call for a new business model that will contribute to all stakeholders and society's wellbeing and achieve economic profitability. The Business Roundtable commitment to stakeholders of August 19, 2019, focuses on the responsibility business firms must assume in their relations with stakeholders.[5]

- Delivering value to our customers. We will further the tradition of American companies leading the way in meeting or exceeding customer expectations.
- Investing in our employees. It starts with compensating them fairly and providing essential benefits. It also includes supporting them through training and education to develop new skills for a rapidly changing world. We foster diversity and inclusion, dignity and respect.
- Dealing fairly and ethically with our suppliers. We serve as partners to other companies, large and small, that help us meet our missions.
- Supporting the communities in which we work. We respect the people in our communities and protect the environment by embracing sustainable practices across our businesses.
- Generating long-term value for shareholders who provide capital allowing companies to invest, grow and innovate. We are committed to transparency and active engagement with shareholders.

The 2020 Davos Manifesto is also very telling (Schwab, 2019):

- Stakeholders' capitalism rests on private corporations as trustees of the society
- A corporation is not just a profit-seeking entity but also a social organism
- A purely profit-seeking behavior caused shareholder capitalism to become increasingly disconnected from the real economy
- The Davos Manifesto describes a firm's principal responsibilities toward its stakeholders
- Companies should pay their fair share of taxes, show zero tolerance for corruption, uphold human rights throughout their global supply chains and advocate for a competitive level playing field – particularly in the *platform economy.*
- All companies should work with other stakeholders to improve the state of the world they are operating. It should be their ultimate purpose. *Shared value creation* includes *environmental, social and governance* goals as a complement to standard financial metrics.

The proposal in this chapter for building a Human Centered Organizational Culture rests on three pillars: the wellbeing of employees, fair and balanced relationships with stakeholders and embracing the common good (Majluf & Abarca, 2021; Lepeley, 2021).

Wellbeing of Employees

Human centered organizations provide *quality jobs*. Just offering job opportunities is not enough. Quality jobs focus on three dimensions: the working conditions, the organizational climate and very importantly, the meaning of work.

Working Conditions

A good job must simultaneously contribute to enhance the company's earnings and the person's material and spiritual needs. To get people's engagement, they must have a sense of achievement and feel that their work is worthwhile. They must appreciate the result of their effort and be proud of what they do. Issues such as product quality, customer satisfaction and creativity of solutions are all relevant matters.

Perhaps the essential theme included in the working conditions is the demand for fair remuneration. It is not easy to discern because it must balance people's needs and legitimate aspirations with the company's real possibilities.

Another issue of high relevance is occupational health and safety. It requires the company to control work risks and offer comfortable and attractive spaces to operate. Also, offering opportunities to develop people's creative, professional and human potential is central. Likewise, opening spaces for participation in information and decisions and giving them autonomy related to responsibility.

To stimulate people's participation in the workplace, they must feel their opinions are valued, even if what they propose is not finally integrated into the final decision. It is a source of great resentment and frustration when not properly considering people's judgments and opinions. They feel that they have no voice in important matters and that their work is marginal.

Promoting autonomy is a very effective way to foster professional development and personal growth. It provides freedom for defining tasks and structuring daily chores, making work more meaningful and generating engagement and motivation.

Organizational Climate

The organizational climate is positively perceived when working conditions support both hard technical and economic aspects of the job and the soft relational issues such as cooperation and friendship.

Friendship is the highest human good in a community (Zarankin & Kunkel, 2019). It is a relationship based on generosity and affection. Friendship is about giving fellow employees selfless support and understanding and conducting relations in a respectful and friendly manner, regardless of differences – people who work side by side in an organization care for their mutual wellbeing.

Company policies should consider several aspects that are central to creating a positive organizational climate:

1 Justice: Distributive justice (making sure that similarly deserving people get comparable compensation) and procedural justice (measure performance with the same yardstick to provide all people equal opportunities).
2 Recognition: Lavish with generosity and justice recognition for a job well done.
3 Accessible leadership style and caring relationships.
4 Good faith in communication. Based on trust and mutual respect, mainly when a conflict arises.
5 Respect for privacy, being mindful of the life–work continuum.
6 Diversity: The company must open its doors to people of different abilities and charisma, without arbitrary discrimination.
7 Organizational support: For the achievement of personal and group goals.

Meaning of Work

The first challenge of all human centered leaders is to provide meaningful work for their employees. They make clear that even jobs with lower levels of responsibility contribute to advancing the institution's purpose and have a long-lasting impact on the organization.

Directly observing the impact of work on other people's lives is a profound source of meaning. Knowing that work has a purpose beyond oneself gives the job a dimension of altruism and spirituality. Meaningful work is more relevant than salary, career development opportunities or the conditions of employment.

There is a clear and unavoidable ethical dimension in the management of organizations because management decisions affect people's wellbeing. Finding meaning at work gives sense to life. When organizations are *a good place to work*, they attract, retain and motivate the needed employees to build a sustainable future. In this way, they create a workplace where human beings can flourish and prosper. It is beneficial for people and organizations.

Just Relationships with All Stakeholders

Human centered organizations make great efforts to meet all stakeholders' economic, social and environmental expectations and establish equitable relations. Their perception of being fairly treated by the company is essential. The ethics code reveals the firm's commitment to building relationships focused on the wellbeing of stakeholders. A typical ethics code includes the following subjects.

Relationships with Employees

The critical role of employees' wellbeing previously discussed highlights the importance of engagement, a relationship based on fair wages, a shared project that gives meaning to work and quality jobs that allow personal development. Also, sharing information openly, building trust and handling conflicts effectively as learning opportunities are relevant characteristics. These activities, focused on promoting employees' wellbeing, nurture an organizational culture that fosters diversity and inclusion barring all forms of discrimination.

Relationships with Customers

The organization focuses on meeting or exceeding customer expectations delivering excellent products and services at a fair price and addressing their claims in a timely and effective manner. Personal relationships with customers are friendly and caring, respecting their dignity and values. Moreover, they adhere to truthful advertising and commit to open and honest communications. And they write business contracts that are fair and easy to understand, never taking advantage of a business relationship.

Relationships with Suppliers

The organization seeks to establish an ethical relationship with suppliers based on fairness, respect and shared benefits. An ethical relationship between the organization and suppliers is free from undue pressure, litigation and conflicts of interest. Policies, bidding processes and contract management are nondiscriminatory. The relationship implies a mutual commitment based on jointly honoring obligations. On the one hand, the supplier must fulfill the order for products and services as promised in the contract, on schedule, and in the stated amount and quality. On the other, the organization deals with the supplier fairly and pays on time. When meeting these conditions, the relationship benefits both parties: the supplier becomes a *strategic partner*, and the organization gets a dependable supplier that helps the business firm create value and meet the commitments in its mission.

Relationships with the Community

An organization that is an exemplary corporate citizen embraces sustainable practices and actively contributes to the development and flourishing of the communities where they work. It assumes its responsibility in the care and preservation of the environment, complies strictly with the law and pays its fair share of taxes. It integrates into the community by opening communication channels to assess the population's real needs and the social, economic and environmental impact of their actions. It actively participates in areas of interest to the community, facilitates social integration and looks for people's wellbeing. Activities for promoting culture, research and quality of education contribute to a politically, socially and economically healthy country. And finally, it encourages employees to adopt a healthy lifestyle and participate in community affairs.

Relationships with Professional Shareholders

Shareholders require professional managers to act responsibly, keep the law and manage for long-term value generation. They also expect to get a fair return for the resources invested and the risk taken. Managers must actively engage with shareholders and provide them complete and transparent information on the firm's businesses and activities. They must acknowledge that they are the custodian of the resources entrusted to them by a heterogeneous group of shareholders comprised of institutional and individual investors.

Embracing the Common Good

As never before, the pandemic makes us experience a contradictory feeling of isolation at home and unity with humanity. We have the pressing need to feel other people's presence, relating to them and spending time together.

Social networks have made possible a massive exchange of positive messages, collaborative musical projects while apart and a thousand other manifestations that make us feel united. Mysteriously, the feeling is that we are all one. The pandemic once again *uncovered that (blessed) common bond, of which we cannot be deprived: our brotherly belonging.*[6] It happens because we are social beings closely linked by our human nature. The wellbeing of other human beings is important to us. Personal benefits cannot be achieved by harming other people or at the expense of the common good. We all need to be aware that each of our actions, even the most personal or insignificant ones, has a social and environmental impact. We need to cultivate our individuality without suppressing our imperative need to be part of organizations and groups. We must be unique and independent beings and, at the same time, be part of a community of people.

The Common Good in Business Firms

The most relevant aspect in an organizational culture, where there are so many actors involved, is the advancement of a working community aimed at the common good. Although companies must maximize economic value to shareholders if they want to be sustainable, committing all efforts and resources to achieve the common good is the best way to meet the high human and economic expectations and demands placed on business firms.

The starting point is transparency and self-control of its actions and decisions. A successful company does not tolerate any form of corruption or abuse in any area of activity. When these companies get aware of improper conduct with customers, suppliers, employees, shareholders or the community, they quickly report the situation and apply exemplary sanctions.

To accomplish this pursuit, companies must create institutions, establish procedures and define rules to assess and regulate ethical conduct. Implementing ethical and compliance programs is the customary way to institutionalize policies that promote proper behavior among employees across an organization. It is manifested in the Code of Ethics, reporting lines, Ethics Committees and other practices. But even more important is to have a Corporate Social Responsibility (CSR) system and a Culture of Care that highlight the company's social role and the person's central importance. It is crucial to weigh the impact that acts have on people's wellbeing in any decision taken. The aim is to create an organizational culture that fosters the *economic optimum* and the *ethical optimum* simultaneously. It is the only way to ensure that moral and not economic criteria are the ones that shape the pattern of action of an organization.

Closing Comments

A company only dedicated to maximizing its profit cannot simultaneously maximize the common good that benefits everyone. The company must ensure that it works to create wellbeing for all stakeholders in addition to achieving an economic return.

The common good is closely linked to respect for the person and the integral promotion of their fundamental rights. A socially responsible organization contributes to people's wellbeing in many ways, including providing essential goods and services such as food, housing, education, health, work and mobilization. Also, important factors in wellbeing are taking care of the environment for future generations, controlling the carbon imprint, avoiding discharge of pollutants and responsible use of natural resources, such as water and energy. Finally, an issue that needs careful attention is creating quality jobs and focusing on all employees' safety and security.

A human centered company is respected and admired by people because it is fair with all stakeholders.

- It offers employees fair compensation
- It charges reasonable prices to customers and suppliers and transparently relates to them
- It pays its fair share of taxes
- It ensures shareholders an appropriate risk-adjusted return for their investment and provides ample information to them
- It integrates with the community, actively contributing to its progress
- It takes the utmost care in its relationship with other companies to ensure the fairness of its actions, avoiding questionable business practices.

In short, the central point is to recognize that management is not only an economic, technical or legal challenge, but it is primarily a social and ethical challenge. The optimal Human Centered Organizational Culture is enhanced when a business creates successful bonds of trust with all relevant stakeholders, as a necessary condition for long-term sustainability and profitability. It is also the best way to make a substantial contribution to the common good and the construction of a Culture of Care.

Notes

1 https://www.worldbank.org/en/research/brief/human-development
2 http://hdr.undp.org/en/content/human-development-index-hdi
3 https://worldhappiness.report/ed/2020/
4 https://www.weforum.org/agenda/2019/12/davos-manifesto-2020-the-universal-purpose-of-a-company-in-the-fourth-industrial-revolution/
5 https://www.businessroundtable.org/business-roundtable-redefines-the-purpose-of-a-corporation-to-promote-an-economy-that-serves-all-americans
6 Homily of Pope Francis at the Urbi et Orbis blessing, March 27, 2020. Accessed on http://www.vatican.va/content/francesco/en/homilies/2020/documents/papa-francesco_20200327_omelia-epidemia.html

References

Navarro, J. A. (2020). Coronavirus: La hora de la filosofía, *Babelia, El País*, 1 April. Available at: https://elpais.com/cultura/2020/03/31/babelia/1585676259_109937.html (Accessed: 04 04 2020)

Authers, J. (2020). How coronavirus is shaking up the moral universe, *Bloomberg*, 29 March. Available at: https://www.bloomberg.com/opinion/articles/2020-03-29/coronavirus-pandemic-puts-moral-philosophy-to-the-test (Accessed: 02 04 2020)

Bower, J. L., Leonard, H. B., & Paine, L. S. (Sep. 2011). Global capitalism at risk: What are you doing about it? *Harvard Business Review*, *89*(7), 105–112.

Cortina, A. (2020). La sociedad va a cambiar radicalmente después de esta crisis, *La Vanguardia*, March 25. Available at: https://www.lavanguardia.com/local/valencia/20200325/4891567297/adela-cortinas-sociedad-cambiar-radicalmente-despues-crisis-coronavirus.html (Accessed: 11 04 2020)

Jauregui, R. (2020). ¿Un capitalismo diferente?, *Ethic*, 30 March. Available at: https://ethic.es/2020/03/un-capitalismo-diferente/ (Accessed: 02 04 2020)

Lepeley, M.T. (2017a). *Human Centered Management. The 5 Pillars of Organizational Quality and Global Sustainability*. UK: Routledge.

Lepeley, M. T. (2017b). Bhutan's Gross National Happiness. An approach to human centred sustainable development. *South Asian Journal of Human Resource Management*, *4*(2), 174–184.

Lepeley, M. T. (2021). Soft Skills: The lingua franca of Human Centered Management. In M. T. Lepeley, N. Beutell, N. Abarca, P. Essens, & N. Majluf (Eds.). *Soft Skills for Human Centered Organizational and Global Sustainability*. USA: Routledge.

Majluf, N., & Abarca, N. (2021). *The Human Centered Leader: Sensible, Insightful, and Prudent*. USA: Routledge.

Ouyang, H. (2020). I'm an E.R. Doctor in New York. None of Us Will Ever Be the Same. A Covid diary: This is what I saw as the pandemic engulfed our hospitals, *The New York Times Magazine*, 14 April, Updated 27 May. Available at: https://www.nytimes.com/2020/04/14/magazine/coronavirus-er-doctor-diary-new-york-city.html (Accessed: 15 08 2020)

Porter, M. E., & Kramer, M. R. (Jan. 2011). Creating shared value: How to reinvent capitalism and unleash a wave of innovation and growth, *Harvard Business Review*, *89*(1), 62–77.

Sandel, M. J. (2020). Are we all in this together? *New York Times*, 13 April. Available at: https://www.nytimes.com/2020/04/13/opinion/sunday/covid-workers-healthcare-fairness.html (Accessed: 14 04 2020)

Schwab, K. (2019). What kind of capitalism do we want? *Project Syndicate*, 02 December. Available at: https://www.project-syndicate.org/commentary/stakeholder-capitalism-new-metrics-by-klaus-schwab-2019-11 1/ (Accessed: 07 12 2019)

Zarankin, T. G., and Kunkel, D. (2019). Colleagues and Friends: A Theoretical Framework of Workplace Friendship, *Academy of Management*, published online 1 Aug. Available at: https://doi.org/10.5465/AMBPP.2019.10100abstract (Accessed: 15 08 2020)

9 Virtuous Work and Organizational Culture

How Aristotelian Practical Wisdom can Humanize Business

Javier Pinto, Ignacio Ferrero, Germán Scalzo

The Role of Practical Wisdom in Organizational Theory

In the last decades, Aristotelian virtue ethics has experienced a revival (Ferrero & Sison, 2014). We sustain that its application to organizational theory (Nonaka & Takeuchi, 2011, Solomon, 2004; Weaver, 2006) presents good opportunity for understanding practical knowledge of organizations effective to humanize business practices in a way that can overcome the rationalistic and mechanistic paradigm (Tsoukas & Cummings, 1997).

The mechanistic approach to organizational theory emphasizes quantifications of economic thought overshadowing character and virtues through universally applicable rules and algorithms (Statler & Roos, 2006). The approach results in management practices based on a depersonalized theory overlooking the importance of character. Predominant contemporary economic theories emphasize individual freedom exclusively understood as the opportunity to choose from available options and conceptualize individuals as profit-maximizing actors, neglecting, in turn, their freedom to reflect on the purposes and goals of their actions (Moosmayer et al., 2018). In addition, many authors suggest that management education based on this mechanistic approach has widely and uncritically assumed contracted pursuit of managerial technique looking at natural sciences to explain organizational behaviors (Bennis & O'Toole, 2005), at the expense of good judgment and moral responsibility (Morrell & Learmonth, 2015; Rocha & Ghoshal, 2006).

Modern mechanistic tendencies anchored in resource-based imperatives embedded in Human Resource Management are no longer effective (Tsoukas & Cummings, 1997). On the contrary, growing evidence shows negative effects on work engagement and levels of job satisfaction worldwide eroding fundamental principles of wellbeing in human centered organizations that are essential to achieve high organizational performance and productivity. The moral component of the social sciences is needed at the center of organizations. In this line, an Aristotelian approach to modern organizations reinforces the free spirit of people necessary to advance human wellbeing, Human Centered Management and sustainable organizations in inclusive societies worldwide (Lepeley, 2017).

Aristotelian Virtue Ethics essentially implies that individual human excellence, that is, achievement of a virtuous and flourished life, goes hand in hand with the excellence of institutions and thriving societies (Sison & Ferrero, 2015) that promote the common good.

To Aristotle, practical wisdom (*phronesis*) is the virtue of practical knowledge (Statler, Roos, & Victor, 2007), which is put into practice in terms of deliberation (*boulesis*) and decision-making or execution (*prohairesis*) (Aristotle *Nicomachean Ethics* – hereafter *NE* – 1113a, 1140b). The importance of practical wisdom in decision-making is based on its application to the analysis of complex situations, identification of moral content and implications (Roca, 2008) and enhancing practice of a common good which endows organization's members with excellence.

Aristotelian practical wisdom is defined as doing the right thing given a set of particular circumstances, and effectively safeguarding the intended *good* relevant to a given situation through deliberative processes (Melé, 2010, 2012).

Introducing Aristotelian practical wisdom in organizations emphasizes their practical nature. Practical wisdom turns into a conceptual framework explaining organizational activity and development (De Bruin, 2013; Nonaka & Takeuchi, 2011) and supporting working policies (Moberg, 1999; Provis, 2010). Therefore, it contributes to improve understanding what organizations are *teleologically*, explaining the nature of communities being actively reality-oriented toward improvement and achieving higher purposes (*telos*) (Aristotle, *Politics*, 1252b). Following Aristotle, we sustain that the purpose of action is excellence. Therefore, organizations should aim toward excellence and engagement of people who work for it, if the intent is to support their personal development. In other words, organizational excellence is based on how excellent work is envisaged.

From the agent's perspective, orientation toward improvement is described as teleological (*telos*) and proper to every human form of organization or community (Aristotle, *Politics*, 1252a). Aristotle would have identified, *mutatis mutandis*, an organizational end (*telos*) as the final cause why organizations exist. Consequently, the end of any good organization cannot be defined in terms of survival alone (that is, in purely economic terms) but must also include a component of excellence, in addition to the productive and economic means (Koehn, 1995; González & Guillén, 2008). Hence, Aristotelian practical wisdom is driven by its aim to achieve and perfect people's skills and adhere to higher standards of personal excellence (Shotter & Tsoukas, 2014), and the same can be said of organizations in pursuit of excellence.

Practical wisdom, understood as good practical knowledge in action, refers to the habit of acting correctly and it includes the subjective processes of perception and deliberation (Solomon, 1992). It requires integration of organizational reality, characterized by particular facts and circumstances, with the uniqueness of situations fostered by personal actions (Arjoon, 2008; Shotter & Tsoukas, 2014) and grasping the essence of a situation (Nonaka & Takeuchi, 2011), giving meaning and contextualizing specific conditions.

A person with practical wisdom displays skills and habits needed for optimal deliberation how to live a good life and applies practical wisdom to situations with reasoned capacity to act on things that are good and bad for human beings.

Practical wisdom may also be explained as habitual conformity between right thinking and right desire ultimately seen in practical reasoning (Koehn, 1995), i.e., harmony of rationality, emotions and intuitions in decision-making and action processes (Hartman, 2008).

Finally, practical wisdom refers to integrity of one's life – practices, roles, duties and responsibilities – (Solomon, 1992), continuity or identification between one's past and future (Koehn, 1995; Hartman, 2006) and achievement of happiness (Sison, 2014).

Actions carried out according to good practical judgment strengthened character (Koehn, 1995; Hartman, 1998; Solomon, 2003; Whetstone, 2005), and, in turn, is akin to repository of habits enabling people to act in an ethically and correct way (Sison & Ferrero, 2015). Therefore, in a practical approach to organizational activity, the human agent not only contributes to production but also to self-improvement through decision-making and action (Shotter & Tsoukas, 2014; Scalzo, 2018), that are essential to reach standards of excellence. This is, in fact, a key concept when defining the nature of a practical organization, an organization developed in accordance with the principles of Aristotelian practical wisdom in terms of proper organizational end (*telos*) aims fostering its members to personal excellence.

Virtuous Work and Ethical Culture

The different approaches to the nature of organizations and their *telos* imply different definitions of work, according to the organizations' approaches toward excellence or toward mere productivity (Sison & Ferrero, 2015). We claim that Aristotelian practical wisdom applied to organizational theory offers an original definition of work resulting in a conception of organization as a community of work. In this section, we show how this idea of work contributes to a virtuous organizational culture.

Aristotle describes work as an inherently human function, *ergon*, which may or may not be perfective, and characterized by excellence to such extent that it involves actions that are productive and supported by reason and therefore are ordered according to reason (Gomez-Lobo,

1989). However, not every form of work can be performed as *ergon*. Aristotle conceives of a potential disassociation between the unity of thought and action, when one worker carries out another's original idea and not the personal idea.

Industrialization as a form of mechanization led to productive processes based on repetitive tasks and mechanical movements, removing practical and perfective dimensions of productive tasks from employees in favor of increased productivity. It implies a definition of work as mere production and a concomitant faith in scientific laws and replicable techniques. It aims to ascertain the best method for work processes reconceived in terms of temporal machines and workers who are exclusively understood as instruments to be used for the operation of these machines (Breen, 2012). Consequently, as many authors have argued, it affects workers' ability to attain personal flourishing (Kanungo, 1992) because it reduces or hinders deliberation for the sake of production. In fact, employees that only follow operational protocols and focus on isolated contributions to a process are barred from using their practical wisdom and consequently they impair their personal development at work (Ferrero & Calderón, 2013). Organizations that promote this method are incompatible with a community of work aiming at excellence.

To Aristotle, excellent work is understood as a perfective action (Pinto-Garay, 2015) that implies personal deliberation using practical wisdom and valuing production not only based on material productivity but also and mainly on personal thriving and work excellence. Deliberation can be materialized as a form of shared and cooperative work in terms of decision-making (Schwartz & Sharpe, 2006) and shared-deliberation (MacIntyre, 2016) aimed to thriving of the community of work. When workers deliberate, they apply their practical wisdom in execution and production, therefore, they attain virtues implicit in the notion of self-realization, choosing a good end and directing production in accordance with those objectives (Murphy, 1993). The purpose of productive activities is performance aligned with the agent's personal or moral development, acquisition of knowledge, skills and habits as ultimate purpose of the most valuable output (Sison, Ferrero, & Guitián, 2016). This is a way to achieve personal excellence.

When personal excellence as an organizational end is achieved, the organization demonstrates good corporate character (Moore, 2005) and attains the common good that is embedded in the community, the organization and all its members.

Communities of Work and the Common Good

From an Aristotelian perspective, all economic and productive organizations must aim toward becoming a community of work (Solomon,

1992; Sison & Fontrodona, 2013), an organization that is productive for the benefit, excellence and virtue of those who work there. Indeed, when an organization's resources, economic–financial means, culture and policies are oriented toward its members' personal development, it is said that the organization works for *the common good* (Sison & Fontrodona, 2012; 2013).

The common good is a manifest for all communities' material, cultural and organizational aspects (Finnis, 1980). The organization's common good is wider than just the attainment of the material conditions necessary for undertaking a joint activity and the coordination of actions to ensure profit; in addition, and more importantly, the common good emerges from the contribution of the actions of each member and their personal development.

Organization achieve excellence in the form of common good when their members participate, engaged in collaborative and productive tasks contributing to personal and organizational development, fulfillment and flourishing (Pinto-Garay, 2015). In fact, participation in any community bears the historical development of norms and standards and possibilities that individuals, who participate in the community, can debate those norms and standards and can change them through a process of collective deliberation.

Solomon sustains that the Aristotelian understanding of the firm is to be part of a community and debating that the prevailing norms are inextricable links (Solomon, 1992). Participation and deliberation go together. Handy also explains that when promoting freedom and personal initiative effectively, managers need to avoid paternalistic approaches that monopolize procedures, activities and operations that deprive employees of choice, initiative and any other form of responsibility (Handy, 1999).

Following Aristotle, MacIntyre remarks that the end of informing about workers' activity is achieved through shared deliberation and decisions. Accordingly, it matters that people understand what they are doing and that their standards match their own not those imposed by managerial control because all shared the same direction toward the common good (MacIntyre, 2016).

The common good of the organization is a practice performed by the people who work in a corporation. Without a concept of virtuous work, the common good and excellence of the organization and the importance of practical knowledge cannot be integrated in the Aristotelian organizational theory.

An organization's common good is based on practical wisdom and materializes in the firm's policies and culture when based on common deliberation empowering employees (Spreitzer 2008), integrating ethics into organizational theory through policies affecting workers' participation (Wicks & Freeman, 1998). Good management policies entail managers sharing power with employees, where power is understood as the possession of formal authority or control over organizational resources (Kanungo, 1992). Policies therein are formulated according to the following: (i) Managers and all those who work for the organization need to be engaged in organizational decision-making (Moriarty, 2009); (ii) engagement should be oriented toward organizational effectiveness in production; and (iii) employees need to have certain degree of autonomy without diminishing management's authority or disorganizing production (Conger & Kanungo, 1988).

This approach fosters employee engagement, productivity and commitment to the organization, all of which are certain to enhance the organization's overall effectiveness (Conger & Kanungo, 1988).

Beneath this description of organizational policies rests a definition of the organization as a community sharing what is good for every member and for the organizational development. Work based on practical wisdom implies seeking to be effective, efficient and virtuous at the same time. Consequently, virtuous work policies are justified if they positively influence the firm's productivity and competitiveness (Drake & Schlachter, 2008). In this sense, Nonaka, Toyama, & Hirata, (2008) argue that reformulating management theory based on Aristotelian ethics opens up a better understanding of action within organizations as integration of practical knowledge and production. If using practical wisdom does not help efficiency in production, its role in organizations is meaningless.

To sum up, based on Aristotelian practical wisdom, organizations are a community of work whose main goal (*telos*) is personal thriving for all community members through shared-deliberative work. Practical organizational theory is teleological and oriented toward fostering virtue in its members through decision-making opportunities during the productive process and, therefore, organization excellence is reflected as the organizational common good.

Conclusion

To overcome the rationalistic paradigm of organizational theory, we have considered Aristotelian practical wisdom as an opportune path toward developing a more comprehensive understanding of organizations. The concept of work excellence gives a more complete explanation of Aristotelian practical knowledge means in organizational theory. Aristotelian practical wisdom explains organizations deepening understanding and incorporating new features of personal work in organizational contexts.

Specifically, Aristotelian practical wisdom provides a conceptual framework to address key considerations of organizational theory: (i) provides a consistent description of what organizations are in terms of a community of work, (ii) explains the nature of practical knowledge needed in organizations in terms of work as deliberative and participative in production processes. Aristotelian practical knowledge sustains a coherent organizational theory based on practical work with deeper consideration of practical organization defined as a community of work.

The nature of the practical organization finds its definition in the articulation of a common goal, the need for productivity and the search for personal excellence of all its members as the main source of excellent work. These features are integrated with practical wisdom as the keystone of every organization that seeks to thrive individually and collectively. The practical organization is by definition a community of deliberative production aimed at achieving its members' personal development through productive tasks.

If the organization reaches excellence, it is because its members have attain excellence as they act for the sake of corporate development in a cooperative fashion (Kennedy, 2006), providing goods and services efficiently and profitably (Melé, 2012) through productive activities that flourish encouraging the development of virtue in each member of the community (Sison & Fontrodona, 2012).

References

Aristotle. (1995a). Nicomachean ethics. In J. Barnes (Eds.). *The Complete Works of Aristotle*. Princeton: Princeton University Press.

Aristotle. (1995b). The Politics. In J. Barnes (Eds.). *The Complete Works of Aristotle*. Princeton: Princeton University Press.

Arjoon, S. (2008). Reconciling situational social psychology with virtue ethics. *International Journal of Management Reviews*, *10*(3), 221–243.

Bennis, W. G., & O'Toole, J. (2005). How business schools lost their way. *Harvard Business Review*, *83*(5), 96–104.

Breen, K. (2012). Reason, production, and rival visions of working life. In R. Edmondson & K. Hülser (Eds.). *Politics of Practical Reasoning: Integrating Action, Discourse and Argument*. Lanham: Lexington Books.

Conger, J. A., & Kanungo, R. N. (1988). The empowerment process: Integrating theory and practice. *Academy of Management Review*, *13*(3), 471–482.

De Bruin, B. (2013). Epistemic virtues in business. *Journal of Business Ethics*, *113*(4), 583–595.

Drake, M., & Schlachter, J. (2008). A virtue-ethics analysis of supply chain collaboration. *Journal of Business Ethics*, *82*(4), 851–864.

Ferrero, I., & Calderón, R. (2013). The ethical dimension of industrial mass production: The role of transitive motivation. *Journal of Markets and Morality*, *16*(2), 529–541.

Ferrero, I., & Sison, A. J. G. (2014). A quantitative analysis of authors, schools and themes in virtue ethics articles in business ethics and management journals 1980–2011. *Business Ethics: A European Review*, *23*(4), 375–400.

Finnis, J. (1980). *Natural Law and Natural Rights*. Oxford: Oxford University Press.

González, T. F., & Guillén, M. (2008). Organizational commitment: A proposal for a wider ethical conceptualization of 'normative commitment'. *Journal of Business Ethics*, *78*(3), 401–414.

Gomez-Lobo, A. (1989). The ergon inference. *Phronesis*, *34*(2), 170–184.

Handy, C. (1999). Subsidiarity is the word for it. *Across the Board*, *36*(6), 7–8.

Hartman, E. M. (1998). The role of character in business ethics. *Business Ethics Quarterly*, *8*(3), 547–559.

Hartman, E. M. (2006). Can we teach character? An Aristotelian answer. *Academy of Management Learning and Education*, *5*(1), 68–81.

Hartman, E. M. (2008). Socratic questions and Aristotelian answers: A virtue-based approach to business ethics. *Journal of Business Ethics*, *78*(3), 313–328.

Kanungo, R. N. (1992). Alienation and empowerment: Some ethical imperatives in business. *Journal of Business Ethics*, *11*(5-6), 413–422.

Kennedy, R. G. (2006). Corporations, common goods, and human persons. *Ave Maria Law Review*, *4*, 1.

Koehn, D. (1995). A role of virtue ethics in the analysis of business practice. *Business Ethics Quarterly*, *5*(3), 533–539.

Lepeley, M. T. (2017). *Human Centered Management. The 5 Pillars of Organization Quality and Global Sustainability*. New York, NY: Routledge.

MacIntyre, A. (2016). *Ethics in the Conflicts of Modernity: An Essay on Desire, Practical Reasoning, and Narrative*. UK: Cambridge University Press.

Melé, D. (2010). Practical wisdom in managerial decision making. *Journal of Management Development*, *29*(7/8), 637–645.

Melé, D. (2012). The firm as a "community of persons": A pillar of humanistic business ethos. *Journal of Business Ethics*, *106*(1), 89–101.

Moberg, D. J. (1999). The big five and organizational virtue. *Business Ethics Quarterly*, *9*(2), 245–272.

Moore, G. (2005). Corporate character: modern virtue ethics and the virtuous corporation. *Business Ethics Quarterly*, *15*(4), 659–685.

Moosmayer, D. C., Waddock, S., Wang, L., Hühn, M. P., Dierksmeier, C., & Gohl, C. 2018. *Leaving the road to Abilene: A pragmatic approach to addressing the normative paradox of responsible management education Journal of Business Ethics*, *4*, 1–20.

Morrell, K., & Learmonth, M. (2015). Against evidence-based management, for management learning. *Academy of Management Learning and Education*, *14*(4), 520–533.

Moriarty, J. (2009). Participation in the workplace: Are employees special?. *Journal of Business Ethics*, *93*, 373–384.

Murphy, J. B. (1993). *The Moral Economy of Labor: Aristotelian Themes in Economic Theory*. New Haven: Yale University Press.

Nonaka, I., & Takeuchi, H. (2011). The wise leader. *Harvard Business Review*, *89*(5), 58–67.

Nonaka, I., Toyama, R., & Hirata, T. (2008). *Managing Flow: A Process Theory of the Knowledge-Based Firm*. New York: Palgrave Macmillan.

Pinto-Garay, J. (2015). The concept of work in a common good theory of the firm. *Business and Professional Ethics Journal*, *34*(1), 45–70.

Provis, C. (2010). Virtuous decision making for business ethics. *Journal of Business Ethics*, *91*(1), 3–16.

Roca, E. (2008). Introducing practical wisdom in business schools. *Journal of Business Ethics*, *82*(3), 607–620.

Rocha, H. O., & Ghoshal, S. (2006). Beyond self-interest revisited. *Journal of Management Studies*, *43*(3), 585–619.

Scalzo, G. (2018). Virtues and the common good in production. In A. Sison, I. Ferrero, & G. Guitián (Eds.). *Virtuous Business for the Common Good (82-98)*. London and New York: Routledge.

Schwartz, B., & Sharpe, K. E. (2006). Practical wisdom: Aristotle meets positive psychology. *Journal of happiness studies*, *7*(3), 377–395.

Shotter, J., & Tsoukas, H. (2014). Performing phronesis: On the way to engaged judgment. *Management Learning*, *45*(4), 377–396.

Sison, A. J. G. (2014). *Happiness and Virtue Ethics in Business*. UK: Cambridge University Press.

Sison, A. J. G., & Ferrero, I. (2015). How different is neo-Aristotelian virtue from positive organizational virtuousness?. *Business Ethics: A European Review*, *24*, S78–S98.

Sison, A. J. G., Ferrero, I., & Guitián, G. (2016). Human dignity and the dignity of work: Insights from Catholic social teaching. *Business Ethics Quarterly*, *26*(4), 503–528.

Sison, A. J. G., & Fontrodona, J. (2012). The common good of the firm in the Aristotelian-Thomistic tradition. *Business Ethics Quarterly*, *22*(2), 211–246.

Sison, A. J. G., & Fontrodona, J. (2013). Participating in the common good of the firm. *Journal of Business Ethics*, *113*(4), 611–625.

Solomon, R. C. (1992). Corporate roles, personal virtues: An Aristotelian approach to business ethics. *Business Ethics Quarterly*, *2*(3), 317–339.

Solomon, R. C. (2003). Victims of circumstances? A defense of virtue ethics in business. *Business Ethics Quarterly*, *13*(1), 43–62.

Solomon, R. C. (2004). Aristotle, ethics and business organizations. *Organization Studies*, *25*(6), 1021–1043.

Spreitzer, G. M. (2008). Taking stock: A review of more than twenty years of research on empowerment at work. In J. Barling & C. Cooper (Eds.). *The Sage Handbook of Organizational Behavior. Volume one: Micro perspectives: 54-*72. London: Sage Publications.

Statler, M., & Roos, J. (2006). Reframing strategic preparedness: An essay on practical wisdom. *International Journal of Management Concepts and Philosophy*, *2*(2), 99–117.

Statler, M., Roos, J., & Victor, B. (2007). Dear prudence: An essay on practical wisdom in strategy making. *Social Epistemology*, *21*(2), 151–167.

Tsoukas, H., & Cummings, S. (1997). Marginalization and recovery: The emergence of Aristotelian themes in organization studies. *Organization Studies*, *18*(4), 655–683.

Weaver, G. R. (2006). Virtue in organizations: Moral identity as a foundation for moral agency. *Organization Studies*, *27*(3), 341–368.

Whetstone, J. T. (2005). A framework for organizational virtue: The interrelationship of mission, culture and leadership. *Business Ethics: A European Review*, *14*(4), 367–378.

Wicks, A. C., & Freeman, R. E. (1998). Organization studies and the new pragmatism: Positivism, anti-positivism, and the search for ethics. *Organization Science*, *9*(2), 123–140.

Part III

Disruptions and Change in Human Centered Organizational Culture in Healthcare

10 Healthcare and the Human Centered Organizational Culture during the COVID-19 Pandemic

The Italian Experience

Francesca Dal Mas, Gabriele Romani, Mirko Modenese, Rossella Lucà, Maria Francesca Manca, Maria Ferrara, Lorenzo Cobianchi

Introduction

The Human Centered Management model focuses on the relevance of the wellbeing of people as customers and patients, in the case of healthcare, and workers who use their talent, human capital and skills to produce services as a necessary condition for organizations to attain long-term sustainability (Lepeley, 2017; Massaro, Bardy, Lepeley, & Dal Mas, 2014). Human Centered Management stresses the importance of the wellbeing of workers engaged in the production of services with quality standards to secure the benefits healthcare users seek and deserve (Massaro, Bagnoli, & Dal Mas, 2020). Human Centered Management highlights that satisfied customers and engaged workers are the keys for organizations in all sectors to reach high performance, productivity and long-term sustainability (Dal Mas & Paoloni, 2019; Ochoa, Lepeley, & Essens, 2019). Lepeley emphasizes that organizations attain quality standards and can provide the best service to patients when the wellbeing of workers is central to the organization, and when people are the core in management, economies and inclusive societies (Lepeley, 2017).

The healthcare sector is strategic for the prosperity and the sustainability of society as primarily responsible for the health and wellbeing of the population (Dal Mas, Massaro, Lombardi, & Garlatti, 2019). Human Centered Management principles are critical in the healthcare sector seeking continuous improvement and quality standards that are applied in other industries. Furthermore, in the 21st century and given the level of competition, quality standards need to be a central concern and a critical responsibility for healthcare organizations and the same applies to those in the public or private sector that deliver healthcare to a large diversity of patients in multiple medical fields (Hanson & Barach, 2012).

Adopting the human centered and patient-centered philosophy is a benefit for patients and healthcare worker, but to meet the demands of Human Centered Management is a considerable challenge for the healthcare sector coping with budget constraints (Massaro, Dumay, & Garlatti, 2015), increasing demand for inpatient and outpatient services to an ageing population (Bowser, Saxena, Fraser, & Marshall, 2019), a massive technological shift (Dal Mas, Piccolo, Edvinsson, Skrap, & D'Auria, 2020; Gordon, Perlman, & Shukla, 2017) and a deficit of healthcare professionals (Limb, 2016). The coronavirus – COVID-19 – pandemic that stated to affect people in countries worldwide early in 2020 put intense stress on healthcare management of Italian public health organizations. These agencies had to cope with unprecedented change and number of emergencies while pursuing the principles of a human centered system.

This chapter presents the experience of the Health Agency of Modena Province, Italy, during the COVID-19 pandemic using a case study approach (Yin, 2014). Consideration needs to be given to the fact that the chapter was first written at the beginning of April 2020 while the COVID-19 pandemic was in full effect in a highly uncertain and unpredictable global environment. Italy, Belgium, the UK and Spain were the countries most affected by the pandemic in Europe. Data were collected by healthcare professionals directly involved in the management of COVID-19 pandemic and interpreted by a multidisciplinary team, including mental health, public health, business management and statistics/machine learning scholars.

The COVID-19 Pandemic Context

On December 31st, 2019, the World Health Organization (WHO) office in China reported a variation of pneumonia of unknown cause in the city of Wuhan, China. One month later, the outbreak was declared as a Public Health Emergency of International Concern later named COVID-19 (WHO, 2020a). On March 11th, 2020, the WHO Director-General defined the COVID-19 as a pandemic given the speed of cross-country and cross-continent spread (WHO, 2020b). The usual symptoms of COVID-19 were fever, tiredness and a mild dry cough. An unknown proportion of people can be infected without developing symptoms or feeling unwell. It is estimated that 80% of infected people recover from the disease without needing special treatment or hospitalization, while about one out of six infected subjects develop the disease with high severity as acute respiratory distress syndrome, septic shock, severe pneumonia and eventually multi-organ failure.

Senior citizens and people with pre-existing medical conditions (e.g., high blood pressure, heart problems, diabetes and cancer) are observed to develop the most severe form of the illness (WHO, 2020c), with

5 percent of the total infected needing inpatient services and intensive care unit (ICU).

Italy was seriously hit by the pandemic in terms of the number of deaths. On April 1st, 2020, Italy had experienced more than 105,000 confirmed cases, almost 16,000 recovered patients and more than 12,000 deaths, standing, at the time of writing, as the country with the highest number of people deceased due to COVID-19.

No vaccines were available to combat the coronavirus neither approved drug treatments for the new COVID-19 (Kupferschmidt & Cohen, 2020). Non-pharmaceutical interventions, such as social distancing and full closure, were imposed to schools and non-essential businesses in Italy and in countries around the world. Extreme restrictions of people's movement were imposed by governments, including transportation by air, land, international national and local travel to control spread of the virus. The objective was to protect the most vulnerable subjects and avoid overburden and distress of the healthcare system, to ensure specialized intensive care beds, staff and breathing support machines for those in need.

One of the first challenges was to increase the number of ICU beds for COVID-19 patients, adding new units and converting existing ones to care for patients (Peters, Chawla, & Turnbull, 2020). To ensure resources to confront the emergency, hospitals stopped providing non-essential inpatient and outpatient services. As a result, hospital suspended elective surgical activities (Cobianchi, Pugliese, Peloso, Dal Mas, & Angelos, 2020) and access to healthcare facilities was strictly regulated to reduce workflows in hospitals.

Healthcare personnel usually engaged in high specialty divisions, and physicians in retirement returned to work and were deployed for the care of COVID-19 patients. A rapid reorganization of services, physical areas and processes was adapted to emerging demands (Grasselli, Pesenti, & Cecconi, 2020), trying to ensure the quality of care and safety for patients and for the healthcare staff considering the dramatic circumstances (Barach & Johnson, 2020).

The Modena Health Agency (MHA) COVID-19 Experience

This section describes the experience of the Health Agency of the Modena Province, in the Emilia Romagna region, the second most affected region after Lombardy in Italy at the time of this writing. At the national level, a full reorganization of medical personnel, equipment, resources and processes had to be put in place.

First of all, the management team of MHA, a public healthcare institution, decided to rely on technology to collect, monitor and analyze data collected during the crisis (Dal Mas et al., 2020; Presch, Dal Mas,

Piccolo, Sinik, & Cobianchi, 2020). A web-based dashboard was implemented in March 2020 to collect patients' information across the Modena province. The information included the number of beds available, results of ongoing testing procedures for COVID-19, number of hospitalized and discharged patients. Data were collected from all the hospitals of the province with updates every three hours.

In terms of resources, MHA was able to increase the number of available ICU beds from 44 to 105 reorganizing areas in other medical services, functions or departments. All non-urgent scheduled surgical and outpatient services, including blood drawn, vaccinations, screening and imaging were cancelled. In the first two weeks, MHA sent more than 29,000 text messages for appointment cancellations. Regular post, social media ad daily press releases were used to keep the population informed (Biancuzzi, Dal Mas, Barcellini, & Miceli, 2020; Dal Mas, Biancuzzi, Massaro, & Miceli, 2020; Graham et al., 2006).

Telemedicine (Bowser et al., 2019; Wang, Ng, & Brook, 2020) was used to monitor vulnerable patients, those with severe mental diseases (Starace & Ferrara, 2020), oncologic patients and ongoing pregnancies. Access to hospital facilities was restricted to patients with proved health emergencies. Allowed patients had to ensure proper hand hygiene and use of hand sanitizers and surgical masks. Visible posters and leaflets highlighted recommended protocols of hand gesture and respiratory health and cough etiquette.

Family members and friends of hospitalized patients were not allowed to visit or look after them, and this regulation included patients in terminal condition (Wakam, Montgomery, Biesterveld, & Brown, 2020). Nobody, except specialized personnel, had access to hospitalized patients, could access the ICU or clinical departments in COVID-19 areas. Similar restrictions were in place for other non-COVID-19 departments, such as pediatrics and obstetrics.

Organizational Culture in Crisis

Healthcare personnel underwent specific training on the use of personal protective equipment (PPE) during the pandemic emergency (Stewart, Thornblade, Diamond, Fong, & Melstrom, 2020). The training highlighted who should use PPE, why, when and how. Existing procedures such as handwash, waste disposal and use of disinfectant products were further supervised to assess correct implementations of recommendations. In a short time, healthcare personnel was forced to drastically change the way they related between them and with patients. Organizational culture was in crisis, and deep transformation was necessary to deal with unpredictable levels of uncertainty about conditions and duration of the pandemic.

The available stock of PPE and other devices, such as breathing support machines, had to be increased to meet needs of rising numbers of patients in need. This operation implied that all available regular and extraordinary suppliers were coordinated and became engaged on short notice to face the emergency situation. This included the donations of masks and aprons by local industries, handcrafted masks by local volunteers' organizations and conversion of industrial textile productions to meet PPE needs.

Each hospital had to identify specific routes and procedures to move COVID-19 patients. Outside buildings, temporary filtering areas were created to separate suspected COVID-19 infected people from other patients with emergencies (injuries or strokes). People who resulted positive to COVID-19 virus but had mild symptomatology were sent back home with medication and recommending for self-quarantine.

Community health resources were implemented to avoid inappropriate accesses to the emergency room and to facilitate discharge from the hospital. Primary care providers and the public health department played key roles triaging referrals of suspected COVID-19 cases and handling infected patients, including contacts and monitoring those quarantined and isolated at home. Community volunteers and non-governmental organizations (NGOs) were involved in the care of quarantined patients, senior citizens and people with disabilities, delivering food and medications.

Large numbers of healthcare professionals involved in the crisis had to stay away from their homes and find alternative temporary housing for long periods of time to protect family members. The Health Agency established agreements with local entrepreneurs and hotels to provide accomodation to healthcare professionals at no expenses.

Medical doctors and nurses in specialties such as cardiology, obstetrics, gynecology, elective surgery and neurology were moved to inpatient wards in high need such as respiratory and infectious diseases, internal medicine, or ICU units. Professionals from palliative care units were responsible for communicating and informing family members of hospitalized patients and consulting with colleagues on the management of terminal patients unable to see their loved ones.

Ambulance transportation service was increased and made available for the fast and safe transfer of patients between units, from high to low intensity and vice versa in different hospitals. A helpline was established to offer support to healthcare professionals experiencing psychological or physical distress during the epidemic. Official social media channels and a dedicated COVID-19 page on MHA website were developed and used to distribute information on recommendations, procedures, emergencies services and Questions & Answers. A toll-free hotline was established for citizens and another for healthcare providers with triage or referral process.

Lessons of Human Centered Management Culture Transformation in a Crisis

The analysis conducted by our multidisciplinary team allowed us to learn from this experience that organizational aspects proved to be central to expedite management during the COVID-19 emergency, ensuring quality of service and safety for patients and especially for healthcare providers. The disruptive pandemic forced a *learning on the job* approach as the only way available to deal with unexpected and unprecedented shocks. Best practices quickly shared with other hospitals and at international level through fast-track publications were coupled with lessons learned from less-than-ideal flows subject to continuous assessment and improvement, which were delivered onsite and online (Garcia Vazquez et al., 2020).

At the time of writing this chapter, the emergency seems partially under control largely due to the effects of enforced non-medical pharmaceutical intervention such as social distancing and the closure of schools and non-essential businesses. Our experience of the MHA during the COVID-19 emergency has helped to identify challenges and learning lessons that allow us to share observations and offer some solutions.

The healthcare ecosystem stands now as a more open system where different stakeholders are cooperating more closely. Managers, clinical staff, patients, entrepreneurs, NGOs and volunteers' associations had to work together to overcome the crisis. The active collaboration fostered and facilitated mutual support and exchange of tools and methodologies. The ability to translate knowledge played a central role in the process. Most realize that only when knowledge is translated effectively, the transfer of relevant information is optimized and sharing is possible and effective. Resilience and agility appear mandatory features aligned with principles of Human Centered Management and the delivery of services in organizations adjusting and reshaping culture under the COVID-19 crisis. That is, resilience in terms of getting strong to bounce back, and agility to overcome disruptions and to move on with the *new normal* dealing with high uncertainty about the future (Cobianchi et al., 2020).

The crisis pressed healthcare personnel to work under new operative strategies never used before. They had to work on co-production of services and increasing patient's engagement as pillars of an upcoming and reshaping healthcare ecosystem. Patients in particular and citizens, in general, lost autonomy as they had to follow recommendations provided by health authorities and clinical staff; with high awareness that their responsibility and collective sacrifice was playing an essential role in problem-solving leading to individual and collective wellbeing as a central feature of the healthcare system that is achieved only if everybody cooperates.

Although the COVID-19 pandemic stands as an epidemiological issue, in reality, many different specializations overlap and had to cooperate.

Virology, medicine, psychology, management, accounting, computer engineering, data management, supply chain, communication and public relations are some of the subjects involved. Hard and technical skills matter, but Soft Skills have been critically important to overcome recurrent situations as people involved in the production of services have to rely more on leadership, change management, teamwork, resilience, agility, communication and ICT skills to help patients (Lepeley, 2021a; 2021b; Yule & Smink, 2020). Training and new techniques, methods and management were increasingly needed. And regardless of the level of education, all individuals had new things to learn either on the job or in a physical or virtual classroom (Garcia Vazquez et al., 2020).

Technology is helpful when people can manage it properly to optimize use because the healthcare system relies heavily on big data analytics. The coronavirus emergency generated massive amount of information that when well managed could lead to practical solutions (Lan et al., 2020) with the aid of artificial intelligence tools (machine/deep learning). Technologies and web-based solutions such as social media channels can represent successful ways to communicate with patients and families.

Sharing is caring. Best practices and lesson learned must be shared, to allow other organizations and institutions to quickly apply successful solutions and avoid mistakes. Rewarding processes can help better management of staff and patients, enhancing quality and safety standards and fostering the wellbeing of all.

Under the lens of Human Centered Management framework and the call for people's wellbeing, several new challenges emerged.

Unmet medical needs arise for several non-COVID-19 patients, who could not get care because their inpatient or outpatient services were suspended. Some of their diseases may have got worse over time (e.g., untreated cancer), some other pathologies could not be diagnosed on time because of the delay in carrying on the necessary tests (e.g., blood collection or screening procedures), leading to the worst prognosis and a more challenging care pathway. Moreover, the dread of COVID-19 induced people with urgent diseases to postpone the request of care. As an example, one of the authors of this chapter (LC) in his surgical activity experienced the death of some patients due to acute peritonitis because of untreated appendicitis. Despite the pain, patients delayed the surgery and avoided to go to the hospital fearing they could be infected with COVID-19.

Most healthcare professionals involved in the emergency had to spend several months under stressful working schedule, performing different tasks they were trained or educated for and often far from their dear ones at home. Furthermore, many of them had to assist patients – not only physically but also psychologically – who died alone without family or friends, and they could solely rely on the consolation of the medical staff looking after them.

The post-COVID-19 pandemic inevitably leads to a new design of the entire healthcare system, which we think should consider the above-mentioned lessons learned. Emergencies such as the COVID-19 may happen again in the future and the healthcare system needs to be prepared. A call for a more comprehensive implementation of Human Centered Management principles and quality and safety standards emerges, to ensure the wellbeing of all the people involved.

References

Barach, P., & Johnson, J. K. (2020). Assessing risk and preventing harm in the clinical microsystem. In J. Johnson & W. A. Sollecito (Eds.), *McLaughlin & Kaluzny's Continuous Quality Improvement in Health Care* (pp. 235–252). Burlington: Jones & Barlett Learning.

Biancuzzi, H., Dal Mas, F., Barcellini, A., & Miceli, L. (2020). *La Traduzione della Conoscenza in ambito medico tra diversi stakeholders. Un caso di studio in oncologia*, Recenti Progressi in Medicina, No.), Forthcoming.

Bowser, J., Saxena, S., Fraser, H., & Marshall, A. (2019). *C66B960B2068A Healthy Outlook: Digital Reinvention in Healthcare*, Armonk: IBM Institute for Business Value, available at: papers3://publication/uuid/00C50A8C-9B9B-49D3-96B8-; https://www.ibm.com/thought-leadership/institute-business-value/report/drhealthcare.

Cobianchi, L., Pugliese, L., Peloso, A., Dal Mas, F. and Angelos, P. (2020), To a new normal: Surgery and COVID-19 during the transition phase, *Annals of Surgery*, available at: https://doi.org/10.1097/SLA.0000000000004083.

Dal Mas, F., Biancuzzi, H., Massaro, M. and Miceli, L. (2020), Adopting a knowledge translation approach in healthcare co-production. A case study, *Management Decision*, In Press, available at: https://doi.org/10.1108/MD-10-2019-1444.

Dal Mas, F., Massaro, M., Lombardi, R., & Garlatti, A. (2019). From output to outcome measures in the public sector. A structured literature review. *International Journal of Organizational Analysis*, *27*(5), 1631–1656.

Dal Mas, F., & Paoloni, P. (2019). A relational capital perspective on social sustainability. The case of female entrepreneurship in Italy. *Measuring Business Excellence*, *24*(1), 114–130.

Dal Mas, F., Piccolo, D., Edvinsson, L., Skrap, M., & D'Auria, S. (2020). Strategy innovation, intellectual capital management and the future of healthcare. The case of Kiron by Nucleode. In F. Matos, V. Vairinhos, I. Salavisa, L. Edvinsson, & M. Massaro (Eds.), *Knowledge, People, and Digital Transformation: Approaches for a Sustainable Future* (pp. 119–131). Cham: Springer.

Garcia Vazquez, A., Verde, J. M., Dal Mas, F., Palermo, M., Cobianchi, L., Marescaux, J., Gallix, B., et al. (2020). *Image-guided surgical e-learning in the post-COVID-19 pandemic era: What is next?*, *Journal of Laparoendoscopic & Advanced Surgical Techniques* , *30*(9), 993–997.

Gordon, R., Perlman, M. and Shukla, M. (2017). The hospital of the future: How digital technologies can change hospitals globally, *Deloitte*, available at:

https://www2.deloitte.com/content/dam/Deloitte/global/Documents/Life-Sciences-Health-Care/us-lshc-hospital-of-the-future.pdf.

Graham, I. D., Logan, J., Harrison, M. B., Straus, S. E., Tetroe, J., Caswell, W., & Robinson, N. (2006). Lost in knowledge translation: Time for a map?. *Journal of Continuing Education in the Health Professions*, *26*(1), 13–24.

Grasselli, G., Pesenti, A., & Cecconi, M. (2020), *Critical care utilization for the COVID-19 outbreak in Lombardy, Italy*, *JAMA*, *323*(16), 122–128.

Hanson, C., & Barach, P. (2012). Improving cardiac care quality and safety through partnerships with patients and their families. *Progress in Pediatric Cardiology*, *33*, 73–79.

Kupferschmidt, K., & Cohen, J. (2020). Race to find COVID-19 treatments accelerates. *Science*, *367*(6485), 1412–1413.

Lan, L., Xu, D., Ye, G., Xia, C., Wang, S., Li, Y., & Xu, H. (2020). "Positive RT-PCR test results in patients recovered from COVID-19. *JAMA*, available at: https://doi.org/doi: 10.1001/jama.2020.2783.

Lepeley, M. T. (2017). *Human Centered Management, The 5 Pillars of Organizational Quality and Global Sustainability*. London: Routledge.

Lepeley, M. T. (2021a). Soft Skills: The language of Human Centered Management. In M. T. Lepeley, N. Beutell, N. Abarca, & N. Majluf (Eds.). *Soft Skills for Human Centered Management and Global Sustainability*. London: Routledge.

Lepeley, M. T. (2021b). Master Soft Skills: The Resilience and Agility Umbrella model. In M. T. Lepeley, N. Beutell, N. Abarca, & N. Majluf (Eds.). *Soft Skills for Human Centered Management and Global Sustainability*. London: Routledge.

Limb, M. (2016). World will lack 18 million health workers by 2030 without adequate investment, warns UN. *British Medical Journal*, *354*.

Massaro, M., Bagnoli, C., & Dal Mas, F. (2020). The role of human sustainability in professional service firms. Evidence from Italy, *Business Strategy and the Environment*, In Press, available at: https://doi.org/10.1002/bse.2528.

Massaro, M., Bardy, R., Lepeley, M. T. and Dal Mas, F. (2014). *Intellectual capital development in business schools. The role of 'Soft Skills' in Italian Business Schools*, Proceedings of the 5th European Conference on Intellectual Capital, Academic Publishing Limited, Reading, UK, pp. 1–8.

Massaro, M., Dumay, J., & Garlatti, A. (2015). Public sector knowledge management: A structured literature review. *Journal of Knowledge Management*, *19*(3), 530–558.

Ochoa, P., Lepeley, M. T., & Essens, P. (2019). *Wellbeing for Sustainability in the Global Workplace*. London: Routledge.

Peters, A. W., Chawla, K. S., & Turnbull, Z. A. (2020). Transforming ORS into ICUs. *New England Journal of Medicine*, *382*(19), 1–2.

Presch, G., Dal Mas, F., Piccolo, D., Sinik, M., & Cobianchi, L. (2020). The World Health Innovation Summit (WHIS) platform for sustainable development. From the digital economy to knowledge in the healthcare sector. In P. Ordonez de Pablos & L. Edvinsson (Eds.). *Intellectual Capital in the Digital Economy* (pp. 19–28). London: Routledge.

Starace, F., & Ferrara, M. (2020), COVID-19 disease emergency operational instructions for mental health departments issued by the Italian Society of

Epidemiological Psychiatry, *Epidemiology and Psychiatric Sciences*, available at: https://doi.org/10.1017/S2045796020000372.

Stewart, C. L., Thornblade, L. W., Diamond, D. J., Fong, Y., & Melstrom, L. G. (2020), Personal Protective Equipment and COVID-19 – A Review for Surgeons, *Annals of Surgery*, *272*(2), e132–e138.

Wakam, G. K., Montgomery, J. R., Biesterveld, B. E. and Brown, C. S. (2020), Not Dying Alone — Modern Compassionate Care in the Covid-19 Pandemic, *New England Journal of Medicine*, available at: https://doi.org/10.1056/NEJMp2007781.

Wang, C. J., Ng, C. Y. and Brook, R. H. (2020), Response to COVID-19 in Taiwan: Big Data Analytics, New Technology, and Proactive Testing. *JAMA*, available at: https://doi.org/10.1001/jama.2020.3151.

WHO. (2020a). Events as they happen. Rolling updates on coronavirus disease (COVID-19), WHO, available at: https://www.who.int/emergencies/diseases/novel-coronavirus-2019/events-as-they-happen (accessed 1 April 2020).

WHO. (Mar. 2020b). WHO Director-General's opening remarks at the media briefing on COVID-19, WHO, available at: https://www.who.int/dg/speeches/detail/who-director-general-s-opening-remarks-at-the-media-briefing-on-covid-19---11-march-2020 (accessed 1 April 2020).

WHO. (2020c). Q&A on coronaviruses (COVID-19), WHO, available at: https://www.who.int/news-room/q-a-detail/q-a-coronaviruses#:~:text=sympto ms (accessed 17 April 2020).

Yin, R. K. (2014). *Case Study Research: Design and Methods.* Thousand Oaks, CA: Sage Publications.

Yule, S. and Smink, D. S. (2020), Non-technical skill countermeasures for pandemic response, *Annals of Surgery*, In press, available at: https://doi.org/10.1097/SLA.0000000000004107.

11 Knowledge Translation during the COVID-19 Pandemic

Francesca Dal Mas, Lorenzo Cobianchi, Daniele Piccolo, Paul Barach

Introduction and Premise

Increasing numbers of organizations in all industries and in countries around the world are advancing the paradigm transformation from the traditional hierarchical, bureaucratic and rigid human-as-resources organizational cultures of the industrial past to the new Human Centered paradigm applied to the Organizational Culture (HCOC) aligned with the demands of the Information Age and the Knowledge Economy. In the 21st century, HCOCs need to be resilient and agile to be able to cope effectively with unavoidable disruptions of the global volatile, uncertain, complex, ambiguous environment (Lepeley, 2017; Ochoa, Lepeley, & Essens, 2019, Lepeley, 2021).

Organizational culture is a core feature in all organizations, regardless of type, size or industry. At the national level and in all cultures, people interact and respond to change. The focus of the human centered culture is people, involved in interactions, collaboration and coordinating actions and behaviors to advance the organizational mission. HCOC is built on the individual responsibility of every member and the collective efforts to explore and find a stimulating workplace for all its members. HCOC is strengthened with mutual trust, affective and effective management of social relationships and harmonious coordination of teams working to achieve high performance, productivity and long-term organizational sustainability.

Although organizational culture is an intrinsic dimension that those who *live it* perceive better than external visitors, in terms of stability, consistency and a certain degree of predictability, the present global environment is pressing organizations to adopt cultures effective to change the status quo and emphasizing innovation and adaptation to changing demands. In the Knowledge Economy, organizational performance is subject to continuous improvement and fast adjustments of culture change. An increasingly common vision is the notion that culture adjusts to change because organizations evolve as social entities, and culture is not only shaped by unity but also disagreements. Organizational culture should help people attain individual and collective goals and provides space to share as well as to contest ideas and values to harmonize the best possible cultural context.

Technology and the information explosion have significant effects in organizational culture. Information is becoming increasingly challenging to manage, difficult to communicate and particularly to transmit ensuring that the person who receives information interpret it in the same way that the person who created/delivered the information intended. This is a central aspect of organizational culture in all industries, but it is most critical in healthcare services responsible for the wellbeing of the population. To manage information effectively, healthcare services have developed a system of Knowledge Translation (KT) (Lemire, Souffez, & Laurendeau, 2013). The purpose of KT is to facilitate and expedite communications aiming to improve the transmission of information and transfer of critical knowledge (Biancuzzi, Dal Mas, Barcellini, & Miceli, 2020).

The material for this chapter was collected and planned during 2019. Then, it was intended to explore the application of KT in healthcare and its effects on organizational culture in healthcare. But the authors ended up writing this chapter in the middle of the coronavirus crisis – COVID-19 pandemic (WHO, 2020). Therefore, the original idea for the chapter was deeply affected by the dramatic events we were living in. Although the original idea was altered by the circumstances, the experience has allowed us to provide first-hand knowledge managing a pandemic in healthcare, which will most likely have strong and permanent effects on healthcare and worldwide.

This chapter on KT in the times of COVID-19 pandemic investigates organizational culture exposed and disrupted by an unprecedented phenomenon of humankind.

The COVID-19 Experience

The beginning of 2020 was characterized by the COVID-19 pandemic, caused by severe acute respiratory syndrome coronavirus 2 (SARS-CoV-2; WHO, 2020), which, at the time of writing (early July 2020), had caused more than 11.4 million cases worldwide, with more than 6 million people recovered and over 554,000 deaths. The experience in countries with early and large-scale community transmission (China, Iran, Brazil, Italy, the US, the UK and Spain) showed that COVID-19 required unprecedented response and mobilization within health systems.

Countries that had not entered community transmission had a narrow opportunity to slow it and prepare health systems to mitigate the impact of the outbreak. One of the reasons some systems were more successful mitigating the COVID impact such as Taiwan and South Korea was the fast introduction of new technologies (Dal Mas, Piccolo & Ruzza, 2020;

Dal Mas et al., 2019; Presch, Dal Mas, Piccolo, Sinik, & Cobianchi, 2020; Wang, Ng, & Brook, 2020), changing the way healthcare professionals work and the competencies required to cope with these challenges, also associated with data analysis (Bowser, Saxena, Fraser, & Marshall, 2019; Dal Mas, Piccolo, Edvinsson, Skrap, & D'Auria, 2020).

Increased life expectancy in developed countries has resulted in an increasing proportion of ageing population (Cheng, Luo, Chiu, & Chen, 2009; Yu, Wang, & Wu, 2015) in high risk of COVID due to high preconditions and chronic diseases in need for comprehensive levels of inpatient and out-patient healthcare services.

Growing expenses and budget constraints in many countries (Dal Mas, Massaro, Lombardi, & Garlatti, 2019; Massaro, Dumay, & Garlatti, 2015) confronted the public sector with increasing costs constraints and demands for hospitals financial accountability. These challenges induced the need for the co-production processes involving producers, healthcare professionals and organizations and users (patients) of healthcare services (Batalden et al., 2016; Biancuzzi, Dal Mas, Miceli, & Bednarova, 2020; Biancuzzi, et al., 2020; Elwyn, Nelson, Hager, & Price, 2019) pressing for patient-centered services and safety and quality standards for all the stakeholders involved (Hanson & Barach, 2012; Leape et al., 2009; Lepeley, 2017; Lopez et al., 2017; Schraagen et al., 2011).

The COVID pandemic amplified the challenges and exacerbated differences among actors based on different competencies, backgrounds, culture, feelings, needs and core aims (Angelos, 2020a, 2020b; Cobianchi, Pugliese, Peloso, Dal Mas, & Angelos, 2020).

In the current environment, KT became an essential item. KT represents a set of methods and approaches to bridge the gaps between knowledge and practice of medicine involving a large diversity of constituencies that includes researchers, clinicians, hospital managers, patients and policymakers (Biancuzzi, et al., 2020; Lander, 2016; Lemire et al., 2013).

The COVID-19 pandemic has been defined as a *social crisis situation, a deadly event, unexpected, an unforeseen disruption causing major human suffering* (Dorasamy, Raman, & Kaliannan, 2013, p. 1834). It requires practical tools to cope with emergencies to help all the people involved, all caregivers, patients and their families. This chapter explores the roles of KT and KT methodologies displayed in the context of HCOC healthcare environment, supposed to be patient-focused, during the COVID pandemic.

KT in Healthcare

KT is getting more attention in many fields based on growing awareness of the importance of synchronization to address the needs of the multiple stakeholders (Lang, Wyer, & Haynes, 2007; Pineault et al., 2010; Savory, 2006). Still, it is most important in healthcare given the nature of the field.

In healthcare, KT is associated with the need to *translate* – interpret, decode, decipher – results of medical research into clinical practice to facilitate the dialogue among caregivers, with patients, institutions, R&D teams, healthcare organizations, public agencies, policymakers and all citizens (Cobianchi et al., 2020).

KT is displaced in different ways to facilitate relations among personnel with different backgrounds and competencies, transmit feelings and goals between caregivers and patients requiring new approaches and techniques to improve communications and knowledge transfer on outcomes and results. KT is essential to improve patients' engagement in their healthcare to facilitate the work of caregivers (Biancuzzi et al., 2020; Biancuzzi et al., 2020). KT represents a strategic tool to improve communications among healthcare institutions, governmental agencies and the community and population at large (patients or citizens).

KT facilitators have been identified. Some approaches are based on the use of Soft Skills and creativity of personnel responsible for patients' care (Massaro, Bardy, Lepeley, & Dal Mas, 2014), others rely on new procedures and technologies depending on the type of stakeholders involved and the group characteristics. The literature stresses how team members learn to connect and transfer knowledge more effectively over time, despite differences using a reservoir of goodwill and trust (Biancuzzi et al., 2020).

KT and COVID-19

The COVID-19 pandemic affected millions of people worldwide, resulting in a high number of deaths, physical deterioration and distress of patients, pain for their families, impacting on large numbers of healthcare professionals. Lack of vaccines to fight a new virus or other effective drug treatments led to the deployment of non-pharmaceutical interventions, including social distancing as one of the few options to limit and control the spread of infection, protect the most vulnerable people (like senior citizens and people with pre-existing conditions) from supporting the healthcare system and avoidance from collapsing (Grasselli, Pesenti, & Cecconi, 2020). Several KT tools and techniques were used to ensure effective KT to manage the crisis.

KT from Scientific Research into Clinical Practice

COVID-19 pushed the scientific community worldwide to study the phenomenon and share results at unheard-of speeds and accessibility. The first studies released concentrated on the epidemiological and clinical aspects. Other studies were concerned with best practices and lessons learned from an organizational perspective (Cobianchi et al., 2020; Peloso, Moeckli, Oldani, Triponez, & Toso, 2020), to help hospitals and healthcare systems to quickly reorganize procedures and policies using the experience of other healthcare producers. Leading medical and managerial journals ensured fast-track, free-of-charge open access to their publications about COVID-19-related topics. Several web portals and social media channels were created to gather and share information quickly, with online conferences, seminars and debates about the pandemic. Multinational companies such as IBM (2020) shared resources free of charge to facilitate the work of scientists studying the virus trying to find a cure. This remarkable shift by publishers and companies was unprecedented supporting KT, but it also raises challenges and issued about publication and circulation of pre-peer reviewed manuscripts due to sensational titles, which were widely quoted by politicians and the media.

KT among Caregivers

Extensive literature highlights that professional groups find it easier to translate and share knowledge among members given their high levels of social trust, cohesion and common aims (Biancuzzi et al., 2020; Cobianchi et al., 2020). Moreover, clinical professionals share common ethos, background and skills, thus transferring knowledge is easier (Graham et al., 2006). However, massive re-organization during the COVID-19 pandemic changed work duties and roles of caregivers (Oluwatomilayo, Panda, Lopushinsky, Varghese, & Brindle, 2020), who, like in the case of wars, had to shift their work and drastically in many instances (Barach, Rivkind, Israel, Berdugo, & Richter, 1998). For instance, surgeons and dermatologists were required to re-tool and up-skill to provide care to COVID-19 patients in intensive care units (Angelos, 2020a; Cobianchi et al., 2020; Peloso et al., 2020). Cancellation of non-urgent surgeries led to unmet medical needs (Cobianchi et al., 2020; Tseng, Roggin, & Angelos, 2020), turning *from patient-centered ethics to public health ethics* (Angelos, 2020a, p. 1).

Extensive hands-on training, including the use of simulators and webinars training (Garcia Vazquez et al., 2020) supported sharing experiences to confront unexpected conditions (Steuffert, Satish, & Barach, 2001). Clinical situations experienced high degrees of disruptions and organizational ambiguity, where the knowledge base and the systems were changing drastically on a daily basis. This uncertain environment boosted the importance of Soft Skills (Lepeley, 2021b, Yule & Smink, 2020) to support fast and accurate problem-solving, sensible leadership and teamwork needed for effective KT facilitation.

KT from Caregivers to Patients

Massive procedural reorganization during the COVID-19 pandemic forced modification of many healthcare and safety operating protocols, including developing new emergency protocols. In most countries, family members and friends of patients were prohibited from entering hospitals and nursing homes to visit their loved ones due to the new isolation standards (Wakam, Montgomery, Biesterveld, & Brown, 2020). This included terminal patients, who had to rely for physical and emotional support exclusively in the clinical staff as the only in-person human connections (Wakam et al., 2020).

The KT tools and techniques solved issues of compassionate care (Wakam et al., 2020) relying on clinical staff's Soft Skills as empathy and compassion (Biancuzzi et al., 2020). Web-based technologies such as online messaging and communication devices such as smartphones and tablets became relevant when patients were ventilated and unable to talk (Wakam et al., 2020). Literature on the topic highlights the need for international guidelines to support clinicians and patients on those issues that became critical during the pandemic (Wakam et al., 2020) and draw lessons from decades of work on the most effective ways to share adverse healthcare outcomes and failure with patients and families respectfully and truthfully (Cantor et al., 2005).

KT from Institutions and Governmental Agencies to the Population

The COVID-19 pandemic required policymakers for taking immediate actions to translate scientific findings to share knowledge to the general public about the virus and steps to protect citizens from being infected, including constraining their movements and liberties. Governmental agencies used media channels, TV and internet live streaming, TV ads, the press and social networks such as Facebook, Twitter and Instagram to plead the case in efforts to promote the importance of social isolation that impacted all non-essential business and economic shutdowns.

Political messages were not always coherent. In Italy, a politician engaged in public handshaking and shared aperitifs in a vibrant Milan underlining that people should not panic with the virus (Pisano, Sadun, & Zanini, 2020) sharing pictures of people gathering in social media channels. A week later, that politician was diagnosed with COVID-19. Globally, several governmental agencies, hospitals and institutions created dedicated official COVID-19 websites to make knowledge available to the population in an effective way employing a simple language. Dedicated social media channels were created by official institutions (for instance, the *Fermiamolo Insieme* – let's stop it together – Instagram page of Lombardy, Italy's most affected Region[1]), and scientists all over the world raised their voices to share simple but useful information.

An example was Prof. Roberto Burioni (Starr, 2020), who used his blog *Medical Facts*[2] to disseminate practical tips and identify fake news. Many celebrities, web influencers and sports stars worldwide made efforts to engage and encourage people to behave as recommended and to raise money to help hospitals and intensive care units acquire equipment and personal protection devices needed by caregivers.

Social media posts were graphics using design elements to transfer the message clearly and smartly (Simeone, Secundo, & Schiuma, 2017). For instance, basic drawings were used to advise people about the importance of correct hand hygiene or the need to wear surgical masks while going out and sheltering at home except for urgent reasons. Remarkably, the population was extremely engaged and cooperative. This stands as a significant example of effective co-production of public services (Batalden et al., 2016) and effectiveness of KT impacting organizational culture. Design elements such as visible posters and leaflets were used by several hospitals and clinics worldwide to advise people about the new rules and procedures, for example, when and how to access hospital departments, sanitizing their hands and wearing mandatory surgical masks. Table 11.1 summarizes the findings of our study.

Table 11.1 Knowledge Translation: Types and Tools

Type of KT	*KT Tool Examples*
Scientific research into clinical practice	Fast track, free-of-charge open access publications Web portals Social media channels Seminars and workshops
Among caregivers	Simulation Online training Soft Skills (e.g., problem-solving, teamwork and leadership)
Caregivers to patients	Empathy and other interpersonal and Soft Skills for compassionate care Instant messaging tools Social media channels
Healthcare institutions and governmental agencies to the population	TV and internet live streaming TV ads The press Social media channels such as Facebook, Twitter and Instagram Testimonials Design elements Posters and leaflets

Source: The authors.

Lessons Learned in the Effective Use of KT in Critical Situations

The international response to the novel coronavirus exposed that healthcare systems around the world are ill-prepared for a pandemic. The spread of coronavirus and the resulting COVID-19 pandemic provided a powerful test about responses of social and governance systems.

Initial successes managing COVID spread are worth sharing because beyond lessons to contain the pandemic have also increased knowledge about pressing challenges related to technology and democracy.

It became clearer that society leaders and healthcare providers need to keep patients informed about evidence and results of experimental therapies and work to enroll more patients in randomized clinical trials. Although the rush to transfer knowledge is laudable, it should not bypass enduring principles in times of high uncertainty and fear to protect patients with valid evidence to fight misinformation.

The spread of the virus and slow rollout of testing meant reporting inaccurate case numbers and death rates, leading to public uncertainty and fear. Experts and officials said that adequate controls are attributed to better reorganization and decision-making, smart use of technology, a central command center and swift decision-making. The pandemic undermined decades of standards, protocols and workflows, which were designed to ensure the best care and safety for all. The pandemic stressed the importance of knowledge transfer and KT continuous improvement cementing a resilient and agile organizational culture able to ensure expected outcomes for all stakeholders in the healthcare system.

Our study identified four critically important KT flows: from scientific research translated into medical practice and among caregivers; from healthcare professionals to patients; and expediting dialogue among political entities and healthcare institutions to inform citizens.

We identified tools and methodologies grabbed from the COVID experience that can foster effective KT that largely depends on the nature and needs of stakeholders. Scientific and highly educated and specialized parties rely more on scientific publications, conferences and workshops. Caregivers relied mostly on their training and their Soft Skills, including leadership, decision-making and teamwork, to translate and share knowledge quickly and implement innovations. Interpersonal skills and empathy played the most outstanding roles during the COVID pandemic as Soft Skills enhancing compassionate care, especially in cases of need for complete isolation in COVID-19 hospitalized patients.

Ultimately, the pandemic uncovered the importance of KT and KT tools to facilitate effective knowledge sharing in healthcare. Indeed, we anticipate how KT will become one of the key pillars in modern healthcare ecosystems. The dramatic COVID-19 experience underlined a call for further studies on the subject as a necessary condition to improve the quality of healthcare worldwide.

Notes

1 Available at https://www.instagram.com/fermiamoloinsieme/?hl=en.
2 Available at https://www.medicalfacts.it/.

References

Angelos, P. (2020a). Surgeons, ethics, and COVID-19: Early lessons learned, *Journal of the American College of Surgeons*, 1–2.

Angelos, P. (2020b). Interventions to improve informed consent perhaps surgeons should speak less and listen more. *JAMA Surgery*, *155*(1), 13–14.

Barach, P., Rivkind, A., Israel, A., Berdugo, M., & Richter, E. (1998). Emergency preparedness and response in Israel during the Gulf War: A re-evaluation. *Annals of Emergency Medicine*, *32*(2), 224–233.

Batalden, M., Batalden, P., Margolis, P., Seid, M., Armstrong, G., Opipari-arrigan, L., et al. (2016). Coproduction of healthcare service. *BMJ Quality & Safety*, *25*(7), 509–517.

Biancuzzi, H., Dal Mas, F., Barcellini, A., & Miceli, L. (2020), La Traduzione della Conoscenza in ambito medico tra diversi stakeholders. Un caso di studio in oncologia, *Recenti Progressi in Medicina*. https://www.ibm.com/thought-leadership/institute-business-value/report/drhealthcare.

Biancuzzi, H., Dal Mas, F., Miceli, L., & Bednarova, R. (2020). Post breast cancer coaching path: A co-production experience for women. In P. Paoloni & R. Lombardi (Eds.). *Gender studies, Entrepreneurship, and Human Capital: 5th Ipazia Workshop on Gender Issues 2019*. New York: Springer.

Bowser, J., Saxena, S., Fraser, H., & Marshall, A. (2019). A healthy outlook: Digital Reinvention in healthcare, IBM Institute for Business Value C66B960B2068 Armonk, available at: papers3://publication/uuid/00C50A8C-9B9B-49D3-96B8-; https://www.ibm.com/thought-leadership/institute-business-value/report/drhealthcare.

Cantor, M., Barach, P., Derse, A., Maklan, C., Woody, G., & Fox, E. (2005). Disclosing adverse events to patients. *Joint Commission journal on quality and safety*, *31*, 5–12.

Cheng, B.-W., Luo, C.-M., Chiu, W.-H., & Chen, K.-H. (2009). Applying cluster analysis to build a patient-centric healthcare service strategy for elderly patients. *International Journal of Technology Management*, *47*(1–3), 145–160.

Cobianchi, L., Dal Mas, F., Piccolo, D., Peloso, A., Secundo, G., Massaro, et al. (2020). Digital transformation in healthcare. The challenges of translating knowledge in a primary research, educational and clinical centre. In K. S. Soliman (Ed.), *International Business Information Management Conference (35th IBIMA)* (pp. 6877–6888). Seville: IBIMA.

Cobianchi, L., Pugliese, L., Peloso, A., Dal Mas, F., & Angelos, P. (2020), *To a new normal: Surgery and COVID-19 during the transition phase*, *Annals of Surgery*, 272, e49–e51.

Dal Mas, F., Massaro, M., Lombardi, R., & Garlatti, A. (2019). From output to outcome measures in the public sector. A structured literature review. *International Journal of Organizational Analysis*, *27*(5), 1631–1656.

Dal Mas, F., Piccolo, D., Cobianchi, L., Edvinsson, L., Presch, G., Massaro, M., et al. (2019). The effects of artificial intelligence, robotics, and Industry 4.0 technologies. Insights from the healthcare sector. Proceedings of the first European Conference on the impact of Artificial Intelligence and Robotics, Academic Conferences and Publishing International Limited, pp. 88–95.

Dal Mas, F., Piccolo, D., Edvinsson, L., Skrap, M., & D'Auria, S. (2020). Strategy innovation, intellectual capital management and the future of healthcare. The case of Kiron by Nucleode. In F. Matos, V. Vairinhos, I. Salavisa, L. Edvinsson, & M. Massaro (Eds.), *Knowledge, People, and Digital Transformation: Approaches for a Sustainable Future* (pp. 119–131). Cham: Springer.

Dal Mas, F., Piccolo, D., & Ruzza, D. (2020). Overcoming cognitive bias through intellectual capital management. The case of pediatric medicine. In P. Ordonez de Pablos & L. Edvinsson (Eds.), *Intellectual Capital in the Digital Economy* (pp. 123–133). London: Routledge.

Dorasamy, M., Raman, M., & Kaliannan, M. (2013). Knowledge management systems in support of disasters management: A two decade review. *Technological Forecasting and Social Change, Elsevier Inc.*, *80*(9), 1834–1853.

Elwyn, G., Nelson, E., Hager, A., & Price, A. (2019), Coproduction: When users define quality, *BMJ Quality and Safety*, *29*(9), 711–716.

Garcia Vazquez, A., Verde, J. M., Dal Mas, F., Palermo, M., Cobianchi, L., Marescaux, J., et al. (2020), Image-guided surgical e-learning in the post-COVID-19 pandemic era: What is next?, *Journal of Laparoendoscopic & Advanced Surgical Techniques*, *30*(9), 993–997.

Graham, I.D., Logan, J., Mb, H., Straus, S.E., Tetroe, J., Caswell, W. et al. (2006). Lost in knowledge translation: Time for a map? *Journal of Continuing Education in the Health Professions*, *26*, 13–24.

Grasselli, G., Pesenti, A., & Cecconi, M. (2020), Critical care utilisation for the COVID-19 outbreak in Lombardy, Italy, *JAMA*, *323*(16), 1545–1546.

Hanson, C., & Barach, P. (2012). Improving cardiac care quality and safety through partnerships with patients and their families. *Progress in Pediatric Cardiology*, *33*, 73–79.

IBM. (2020), Your Computer Can Help Scientists Seeking Potential COVID-19 Treatments, *IBM*, available at: https://newsroom.ibm.com/2020-04-01-Your-Computer-Can-Help-Scientists-Seeking-Potential-COVID-19-Treatments (accessed 18 April 2020).

Lander, B. (2016). Boundary-spanning in academic healthcare organisations. *Research Policy, Elsevier B.V.*, *45*, 1524–1533.

Lang, E. S., Wyer, P. C., & Haynes, R. B. (2007). Knowledge translation: Closing the evidence-to-practice gap. *Annals of Emergency Medicine*, *49*, 355–363.

Leape, L. L., Berwick, D., Clancy, C., Conway, J., Gluck, P., Guest, J. et al. (2009). Transforming healthcare: A safety imperative. *Quality and Safety in Healthcare*, *18*(6), 424–428.

Lemire, N., Souffez, K., & Laurendeau, M. C. (2013). *Facilitating a Knowledge Translation Process. Knowledge review and facilitation tool.* Quebec: Institut Publique de Santé du Quebec.

Lepeley, M. T. (2021b). Master Soft Skills: The Resilience and Agility Umbrella model. In M. T. Lepeley, N. Beutell, N. Abarca, & N. Majluf (Eds.), *Soft Skills for Human Centered Management and Global Sustainability*. USA: Routledge.

Lepeley, M. T. (2017). *Human Centered Management. The 5 Pillars of Organizational Quality and Global Sustainability*. UK: Routledge.

Lopez, C., Hanson, C. C., Yorke, D., Johnson, J.K., Mill, M.R., Brown, K.J., et al. (2017). Improving communication with families of patients undergoing pediatric cardiac surgery. *Progress in Pediatric Cardiology*, *45*, 83–90.

Massaro, M., Bardy, R., Lepeley, M. T., & Dal Mas, F. (2014). Intellectual capital development in Business Schools. The role of 'Soft Skills' in Italian Business Schools. Proceedings of the 5th European Conference on Intellectual Capital, pp. 1–8.

Massaro, M., Dumay, J., & Garlatti, A. (2015). Public sector knowledge management: A structured literature review. *Journal of Knowledge Management*, *19*(3), 530–558.

Ochoa, P., Lepeley, M.T., & Essens, P. (2019). *Wellbeing for Sustainability in the Global Workplace*. London: Routledge.

Oluwatomilayo, D., Panda, N., Lopushinsky, S., Varghese, T.K., & Brindle, M. (2020), COVID-19 – Considerations and Implications for Surgical Learners, *Annals of Surgery*. *272*(1), e22–e23.

Peloso, A., Moeckli, B., Oldani, G., Triponez, F., & Toso, C. (2020). Response of a European surgical department to the COVID-19 crisis. *Swiss Medical Weekly*, *150*(April), w20241.

Pineault, R., Lamarche, P., Beaulieu, M. D., Larouche, D., Jalhay, J. M., Contandriopoulos, A. P. et al. (2010). Conceptual and methodological challenges in producing research syntheses for decisionand policy-making: an illustrative case in primary healthcare. *Evaluation*, *16*(2), 137–152.

Pisano, G., Sadun, R., & Zanini, M. (2020), Lessons from Italy's response to coronavirus, *Harvard Business Review*, available at: https://hbr.org/2020/03/lessons-from-italys-response-to-coronavirus.

Presch, G., Dal Mas, F., Piccolo, D., Sinik, M., & Cobianchi, L. (2020). The World Health Innovation Summit (WHIS) platform for sustainable development. From the digital economy to knowledge in the healthcare sector". In P. Ordonez de Pablos & L. Edvinsson (Eds.), *Intellectual Capital in the Digital Economy* (pp. 19–28). London: Routledge.

Savory, C. (2006). Translating knowledge to build technological competence. *Management Decision*, *44*(8), 1052–1075.

Schraagen, J. M., Schouten, T., Smit, M., Haas, F., van der Beek, D., van de Ven, J., et al. (2011). A prospective study of paediatric cardiac surgical microsystems: Assessing the relationships between non-routine events, teamwork and patient outcomes. *BMJ Quality & Safety*, *20*(7), 599–603.

Simeone, L., Secundo, G., & Schiuma, G. (2017). Adopting a design approach to translate needs and interests of stakeholders in academic entrepreneurship: The MIT Senseable City Lab case. *Technovation, Elsevier Ltd*, *64–65*(July 2016), 58–67.

Starr, D. (2020), This Italian scientist has become a celebrity by fighting vaccine skeptics, *Science*, available at: https://www.sciencemag.org/news/2020/01/italian-scientist-has-become-celebrity-fighting-vaccine-skeptics (accessed 10 April 2020).

Steuffert, S., Satish, U., & Barach, P. (2001). Improving medical care: The use of simulation technology. *Simulation and Gaming*, *32*, 164–171.

Tseng, J., Roggin, K.K., & Angelos, P. (2020), Should this operation proceed? when residents and faculty disagree during the COVID-19 pandemic and recovery. *Annals of Surgery*, *272*(2), e157–e158.

Wakam, G. K., Montgomery, J.R., Biesterveld, B. E., & Brown, C.S. (2020), Not dying alone — modern compassionate care in the COVID-19 pandemic, *New England Journal of Medicine*, doi:10.1056/NEJMp2007781.

Wang, C. J., Ng, C.Y ., & Brook, R. H. (2020), Response to COVID-19 in Taiwan: Big data analytics, new technology, and proactive testing, *JAMA*, doi:10.1001/jama.2020.3151.

WHO. (2020), Coronavirus disease (COVID-19) pandemic, *Health Topics*, available at: https://www.who.int/emergencies/diseases/novel-coronavirus-2019 (accessed 8 April 2020).

Yu, T. H. K., Wang, D. H. M., & Wu, K.-L. (2015). Reexamining the red herring effect on healthcare expenditures. *Journal of Business Research*, *68*(4), 783–787.

Yule, S., & Smink, D. S. (2020), Non-technical skill countermeasures for pandemic response. *Annals of Surgery*, In press doi: 10.1097/SLA.0000000000004107.

Index